THE COMPLETE
CHATGPT JOURNEY
FROM NOVICE TO EXPERT

The Complete ChatGPT Journey: From Novice to Expert

This book is dedicated to my loving wife, Evelina, who has been a constant source of support and encouragement throughout this journey, and to my son, Keoni, whose boundless curiosity and zest for life have been an endless source of inspiration – this book is dedicated to you both. Thank you for filling my world with love, laughter, and the motivation to keep exploring the unknown.

TABLE OF CONTENTS

PREFACE

Welcome, dear reader, to an enthralling journey that will transform you from an AI novice to a ChatGPT master! You're about to embark on a delightful adventure that will not only provide you with the knowledge and skills to excel in the fascinating world of AI-driven text generation.

The objective of this book is simple: I want to empower you with the most comprehensive guide to Chatgpt (currently Version 4), ensuring that you can navigate the ins and outs of this powerful AI with ease, no matter your starting point. From beginners to seasoned experts, this book will be a treasure trove of wisdom, insights, and practical advice.

But that's not all! I firmly believe that the best way to learn is by doing. That's why, at the end of each chapter, you'll find a collection of sample problems that are designed to challenge you and get those creative gears turning. These thought-provoking exercises will invite you to explore, experiment, and play with ChatGPT in ways that you might not have considered before.

I understand that learning something new can sometimes feel daunting, but fear not! I'm here to hold your hand, cheer you on, and guide you through this incredible journey.

So, buckle up and get ready for the ride of a lifetime! ChatGPT mastery awaits you, and we're beyond excited to be part of your transformation. With every turn of the page, you'll uncover new techniques, strategies, and possibilities that will propel you towards AI-driven text generation greatness. Happy reading, and may the ChatGPT force be with you!

CHAPTER 1
INTRODUCTION

Welcome, dear reader, to "The Complete ChatGPT Journey"! Prepare to embark on an exhilarating journey into the fascinating realm of AI-powered communication. With a friendly AI companion by your side, you'll soon unlock the secrets to mastering ChatGPT Version 4 and unleash your full creative potential.

Have you ever imagined what it would be like to have a witty, intelligent, and incredibly helpful sidekick? No, we're not talking about the comic relief character from your favorite movie. We're introducing you to ChatGPT, the groundbreaking artificial intelligence that's poised to revolutionize the way we communicate, learn, and collaborate.

In this lighthearted and informative guide, we'll not only walk you through the ins and outs of ChatGPT but also take you on a rollercoaster of discovery. You'll start by dipping your toes into the basics, gradually progressing to more advanced techniques, and eventually mastering the art of prompt engineering.

Along the way, we'll pepper the path with entertaining anecdotes, thought-provoking examples, and a healthy dose of humor. After all, learning should be fun, right? And just when you think you've seen it all, we'll delve into an array of captivating use cases that will leave you inspired and eager to explore even more.

But wait, there's more! This book isn't just about teaching you the skills; it's about cultivating a mindset of curiosity, innovation, and persistence. We believe in your potential to harness the power of ChatGPT for truly remarkable applications. So, as you flip through these pages, remember to approach each challenge with an open mind and a can-do attitude.

So, dear reader, are you ready to embark on this thrilling adventure into the world of AI-generated text? If so, buckle up and get ready for a wild ride! ChatGPT 4 awaits, and together, we'll transform your ideas into reality. Let the journey begin!

1.1 The Magic of ChatGPT Version 4: A Friendly AI at Your Service

Picture this: You're sitting at your desk, wracking your brain for ideas, and suddenly, as if by magic, a friendly AI assistant pops up, ready to lend a helping hand. Well, my friend, that's precisely what ChatGPT is all about!

ChatGPT Version 4 is the latest and greatest iteration of OpenAI's text-generating wizardry. This phenomenal AI companion is designed to communicate, collaborate, and create content with you, making your ideas flourish like never before.

But what exactly makes ChatGPT so magical? Let's peel back the curtain and take a peek at the wonders that lie beneath:

Conversational Dynamo: ChatGPT takes conversation to new heights, responding to your prompts and questions with coherent, context-aware replies. It's like having a knowledgeable, versatile, and ever-so-eloquent buddy by your side, 24/7!

Prompt Engineering Prodigy: With a little guidance and creativity on your part, ChatGPT can produce a dazzling array of content. From articles and emails to code snippets and beyond, this AI wunderkind is your one-stop-shop for all things text-related.

Learning Machine: ChatGPT has been trained on a vast corpus of human-generated text, gleaning valuable insights into language patterns, context, and style. And while it may not know everything (spoiler alert: it doesn't), it sure knows a whole lot!

Limitless Potential: The true beauty of ChatGPT lies in its incredible adaptability. With your input, it can generate content for a myriad of purposes—brainstorming, summarizing, translating, you name it! The only limit is your imagination.

So, there you have it, the enchanting essence of ChatGPT! As you embark on this exciting journey, remember that this AI companion is here to support, inspire, and elevate your ideas. So, let's put on our wizard hats and dive into the extraordinary world of ChatGPT, where the magic of AI-generated text is at your fingertips!

1.2 Why this book is the Complete guide to Mastering ChatGPT

So, you're eager to conquer the world of ChatGPT, but with so many resources out there, you might be wondering, "What makes this book the complete guide?" Well, hold onto your hats, because we're about to reveal the secret sauce that sets this tome apart from the rest!

All Levels, Unite!: Whether you're a wide-eyed novice or a seasoned ChatGPT pro, this book is crafted to cater to all skill levels. We'll take you on a captivating voyage from the basics to the most advanced techniques, ensuring that you'll emerge as a true ChatGPT master.

The Fun Factor: Who said learning can't be a blast? We've sprinkled this guide with humor, relatable anecdotes, and entertaining examples to keep you engaged, amused, and motivated. Because, let's face it, learning is so much more effective when it's fun!

Hands-On Approach: This book isn't just about theoretical mumbo-jumbo; it's about getting your hands dirty and putting your newfound knowledge to the test! With practical tutorials, sample problems, and step-by-step guides, you'll gain the confidence to tackle any ChatGPT challenge head-on.

Use Case Extravaganza: Prepare to be dazzled by the sheer versatility of ChatGPT! We'll explore a smorgasbord of real-world applications, showing you how to harness the power of AI-generated text to boost productivity, creativity, and innovation.

Mindset Makeover: Mastering ChatGPT isn't merely about acquiring skills; it's about adopting a growth mindset that fosters curiosity, resilience, and experimentation. This book will guide you on a transformative journey, empowering you to approach challenges with optimism and a can-do attitude.

Future-Proof Learning: The AI landscape is ever-evolving, and so should you! This book will equip you with the tools to stay updated on ChatGPT developments, connect with the thriving community, and continue expanding your knowledge long after you've turned the final page.

So, there you have it—the secret recipe that makes "The Complete ChatGPT Journey" an indispensable resource for anyone yearning to unlock the full potential of ChatGPT. Now, let's roll up our sleeves and dive into the mesmerizing world of AI-generated text!

1.3 How to Make the Most of This Fun and Informative Journey

Congratulations, intrepid explorer! You've taken the first step on a thrilling voyage into the world of ChatGPT. But before we set sail, let's make sure you're equipped with a few handy tips to maximize your enjoyment and learning experience:

Embrace Your Inner Curiosity: ChatGPT is an incredible AI companion with a wealth of knowledge and potential. As you navigate this journey, let your curiosity run wild! Ask questions, try new techniques, and don't be afraid to experiment.

Take It One Step at a Time: Rome wasn't built in a day, and neither is ChatGPT mastery! Be patient with yourself as you progress through the chapters. Take the time to absorb the information, practice the techniques, and reflect on your experiences.

Hands-On Is the Way to Go: This book is chock-full of practical tutorials, sample problems, and step-by-step guides. To truly grasp the magic of ChatGPT, roll up your sleeves and dive into these exercises. Remember, practice makes perfect!

Celebrate Your Wins: As you tackle the challenges and triumphs of this journey, don't forget to celebrate your victories—big and small! Each success is a testament to your growth and a stepping stone towards ChatGPT mastery.

Be Kind to Yourself: We all stumble along the way, and that's perfectly okay! Embrace the learning process, and remember that making mistakes is a natural part of growth. Keep a positive mindset, and trust that you'll emerge stronger and wiser with each hurdle.

Connect with Fellow Adventurers: Learning is always more fun with friends! Engage with the ChatGPT community, share your experiences, and learn from the wisdom of others. Together, you'll embark on a shared quest for knowledge and innovation.

Keep the Adventure Alive: The journey doesn't end with this book. Stay updated on ChatGPT developments, explore advanced techniques, and maintain a lifelong love affair with learning. After all, the AI world is ever-evolving, and so are you!

With these trusty tips by your side, you're all set to make the most of this fun and informative journey. So, gather your wits, summon your courage, and let's set forth into the spellbinding realm of ChatGPT. Adventure awaits!

CHAPTER 2

GETTING STARTED WITH CHATGPT

You've successfully completed the first leg of your journey, and now it's time to dive into the heart of ChatGPT. Are you ready to get up close and personal with your new AI companion? Fear not, for we'll be right by your side, guiding you every step of the way!

In this chapter, we'll lay the groundwork for a solid understanding of ChatGPT. We'll start by introducing you to the essentials: what it is, how it works, and why it's such a game-changer. Then, we'll walk you through the process of setting up your ChatGPT account and acquaint you with the user interface—your gateway to the mesmerizing world of AI-generated text.

But that's not all! We'll also provide you with a treasure trove of tips and tricks to help you harness the full power of ChatGPT. You'll learn how to craft effective prompts, decipher the nuances of AI-generated text, and troubleshoot common pitfalls like a seasoned pro.

As you embark on this enthralling adventure, remember that ChatGPT is more than just a tool; it's a companion, eager to collaborate, learn, and grow with you. So, without further ado, let's set sail into the captivating world of ChatGPT and unlock the boundless possibilities that await!

Ready, set, ChatGPT!

2.1 Setting up an Account

Ah, the first step to any grand adventure: getting started! In this section, we'll guide you through the process of setting up your ChatGPT account, which will serve as your passport to the enthralling world of AI-generated text. So, let's dive in and get you up and running in no time!

Choose Your Platform: ChatGPT can be accessed through various platforms, such as OpenAI's official website, API integrations, or third-party applications. For the purpose of this guide, we'll focus on the official OpenAI platform. Head over to OpenAI's website (**https://www.openai.com/**) and navigate to the ChatGPT section.

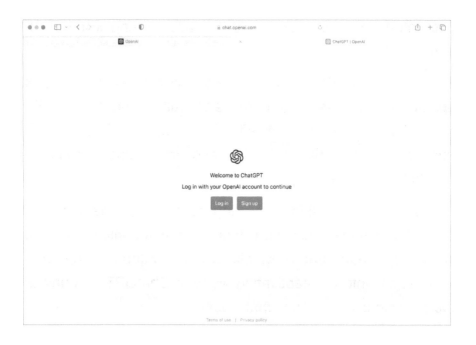

Create an Account: If you're new to OpenAI, you'll need to sign up for an account. Click the "Sign Up" button and follow the on-screen instructions. You'll be prompted to enter your email address, create a password, and provide some basic information. Make sure to verify your email address when prompted, as this will activate your account.

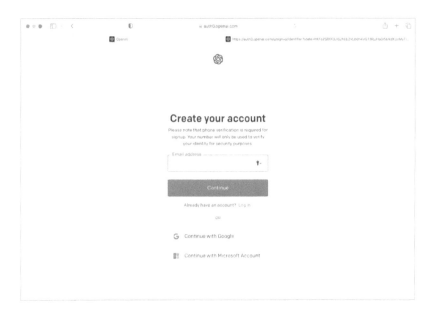

Select a Plan: OpenAI offers various subscription plans for ChatGPT, ranging from free to premium tiers. Each plan comes with its own set of features, limitations, and pricing. Carefully review the available options and choose the one that best suits your needs and budget.

Billing and Payment: If you've opted for a paid plan, you'll need to enter your billing information. OpenAI accepts most major credit cards and supports secure payment processing. Once your payment is processed, your subscription will be activated, granting you access to the fantastic features of ChatGPT.

Account Management: Congratulations! You've successfully set up your ChatGPT account. To manage your account settings, navigate to your OpenAI Dashboard, where you'll find options to update your profile, billing information, and subscription plan. You can also monitor your usage statistics to keep track of your API calls and other activities.

And there you have it! With your ChatGPT account up and running, you're one step closer to unlocking the incredible potential of AI-generated text. In the next section, we'll dive into the user interface, where the real magic begins. So, buckle up and get ready to explore the captivating world of ChatGPT!

2.2 Basic Concepts and Terminology

Before we set off to conquer the world of ChatGPT, it's essential to acquaint ourselves with the fundamental concepts and terminology. This foundation will provide you with the knowledge and confidence to navigate the AI-generated text landscape with ease. So, let's dive into some key terms and phrases that you'll encounter throughout your ChatGPT journey!

Model: ChatGPT is an AI language model created by OpenAI. A model is a mathematical representation of a system, in this case, the language understanding and generation capabilities, trained using a vast dataset of text from the internet.

Token: A token is the smallest unit of text that ChatGPT processes. It can be as short as a single character or as long as a word. The number of tokens influences the complexity of your input, output, and the processing time.

Prompt: A prompt is the input text you provide to ChatGPT to initiate a conversation or request a specific action. Crafting effective prompts is essential for obtaining accurate and relevant responses from the AI.

Response: The response is the AI-generated text provided by ChatGPT based on the input prompt. The quality of the response depends on factors like prompt clarity, model settings, and context.

Context: Context refers to the background information, constraints, or specific details that help ChatGPT understand the nature of the prompt and generate a relevant response.

Perplexity: Perplexity is a measure of the complexity of the text generated by ChatGPT. Lower perplexity indicates simpler language, while higher perplexity signifies more complex and diverse text.

Burstiness: Burstiness refers to the variation in sentence length and structure within a text. Humans tend to write with a mix of short and long sentences, creating greater burstiness, while AI-generated text is often more uniform.

Parameters: Parameters are the adjustable settings within the ChatGPT model that influence its behavior, such as temperature (creativity) and max tokens (response length). Fine-tuning these parameters allows you to optimize the AI-generated output.

API: The Application Programming Interface (API) is a set of protocols and tools that allows you to interact with ChatGPT programmatically, enabling seamless integration with other applications, services, or custom platforms.

Training: Training refers to the process of refining the AI model by exposing it to a vast dataset of text from the internet. During training, the model learns language patterns, relationships, and context to understand and generate human-like text.

Now that you're well-versed in the basic concepts and terminology, you're ready to embark on your ChatGPT adventure with confidence! As you progress through the book and explore more advanced topics, you'll build upon this foundation to master the art of AI-generated text. So, grab your ChatGPT passport, and let's set sail into a world of endless possibilities!

CHAPTER 3

BEGINNER TECHNIQUES IN PROMPT ENGINEERING

Welcome aboard, intrepid adventurer! You've successfully navigated the basics of ChatGPT, and now it's time to unlock the true potential of your AI companion. Prepare to embark on a thrilling journey into the art of Prompt Engineering—a skill that will transform the way you communicate with ChatGPT and elevate your AI-generated text to new heights!

In this chapter, we'll introduce you to a treasure trove of beginner techniques that will empower you to craft compelling prompts and elicit more accurate, relevant, and engaging responses from ChatGPT. You'll learn the secrets of prompt structure, context manipulation, and question phrasing, all while honing your newfound skills through interactive exercises and real-world examples.

But fear not, dear explorer, for we shall guide you through this fascinating landscape with our trademark blend of humor, positivity, and encouragement. We'll provide you with practical tips, accessible explanations, and a healthy dose of fun to ensure that your journey into the realm of Prompt Engineering is as enjoyable as it is educational.

So, gather your wits, summon your courage, and let's set forth into the captivating world of Prompt Engineering. A new chapter in your ChatGPT adventure awaits—let's make it one to remember!

3.1 Crafting Effective Prompts

Ah, the art of crafting effective prompts—a skill that lies at the heart of successful interactions with ChatGPT! In this section, we'll explore the fundamentals of prompt creation, guiding you through the process of constructing clear, concise, and purposeful prompts that yield the desired AI-generated responses. Let's dive in and get those creative juices flowing!

Define Your Objective: Before you start crafting a prompt, it's crucial to pinpoint your desired outcome. Are you looking for a detailed answer, a summary, or a creative piece of writing? Understanding your objective will help you frame your prompt accordingly.

Example Prompts:

Objective: Detailed Answer

"Explain the process of photosynthesis in plants."

Objective: Summary

"Summarize the plot of 'Pride and Prejudice' by Jane Austen."

Objective: Creative Writing

"Write a short story about a time-traveling detective."

Be Clear and Specific: ChatGPT is an incredible AI companion, but it's not a mind reader. To obtain the most accurate and relevant responses, make sure your prompt is clear, concise, and specific. Avoid vague or ambiguous language, and provide enough context to guide the AI towards the desired outcome.

Example Prompts:

[Vague Prompt]:
"Write about nature."

[Improved Prompt]:

"Describe the beauty of a forest in autumn."

Ask Open-Ended Questions: While ChatGPT can respond to yes/no questions, it truly shines when given the opportunity to elaborate. Opt for open-ended questions that encourage the AI to provide detailed and thoughtful responses, allowing you to explore the subject more fully.

Example Prompts:

[Closed Question]:

"Is climate change a major issue?"

[Open-Ended Question]:

"What are the main causes and consequences of climate change?"

We've already covered the importance of defining your objective, being clear and specific, and asking open-ended questions. Now let's continue our journey into crafting effective prompts with more techniques that will elevate your interactions with ChatGPT!

Lead with Context: To help ChatGPT understand the context of your prompt, consider providing a brief introduction or explanation. For instance, if you're asking for a summary of a specific book, include the book's title, author, and a short synopsis before posing your question.

Example Prompts:

[Without Context]:
> "Write an analysis of the main character."

[With Context]:
> "In 'The Catcher in the Rye' by J.D. Salinger, analyze the main character, Holden Caulfield."

Experiment with InstructGPT: Chatgpt includes the InstructGPT feature, which allows you to provide direct instructions to the AI. For example, you can specify the format, style, or tone you'd like the response to follow, giving you greater control over the output.

Example Prompts:

[Without Instruction]:
> "Write a poem about the ocean."

[With Instruction]:
> "Write a haiku poem about the ocean at sunset."

Set Constraints: To further refine your prompt, consider setting constraints such as word count, time frame, or focus area. These limitations help to narrow down the scope of the AI's response, resulting in more targeted and relevant outputs.

Example Prompts:

[Without Constraint]:
> "Describe the history of the Internet."

[With Constraint]:

"Describe the history of the Internet in 100 words, focusing on its invention and early development."

Iterate and Refine: Don't be discouraged if your initial prompt doesn't yield the desired results. The art of crafting effective prompts is an iterative process, so experiment with different approaches, tweak your phrasing, and adjust your context until you strike gold!

Example Prompts:

[Initial Prompt]:

"How does the economy work?"

[Refined Prompt]:

"Explain the basic principles of supply and demand in a market economy."

Learn from Examples: Analyze successful prompts from other users, or even those provided in this book, to gain insights into what works well and what doesn't. By learning from these examples, you'll develop a better understanding of how to craft effective prompts of your own.

With these additional techniques in your toolkit, you're now equipped to become a master of crafting effective prompts. Combine these strategies with your growing knowledge of Prompt Engineering, and you'll be well on your way to unlocking the full potential of ChatGPT. Keep up the great work, and happy prompting!

3.2 Experimenting with Temperature and Max Tokens

In this section, we'll explore two essential parameters in ChatGPT: temperature and max tokens. By understanding and experimenting with these settings, you'll be able to fine-tune your AI-generated responses to suit your specific needs. Let's dive into each parameter and see how they can transform your ChatGPT experience!

Temperature

Temperature is a parameter that controls the randomness or creativity of the AI's responses. A higher temperature (e.g., 0.8 or 1.0) will yield more diverse and creative outputs, while a lower temperature (e.g., 0.2 or 0.5) will produce more focused and deterministic results.

Example Prompts with Different Temperatures:

"Write a creative story about a talking cat and a magical tree. Temperature: 0.8"

High Temperature (e.g., 0.8)
Expect a more imaginative story with unexpected twists, varied vocabulary, and unique ideas.

"Write a creative story about a talking cat and a magical tree. Temperature: 0.2"

Low Temperature (e.g., 0.2)
Expect a more coherent and predictable narrative, with fewer surprises and a narrower range of vocabulary.

Max Tokens

Max tokens is a parameter that limits the length of the AI-generated response. By setting a specific value for max tokens, you can control the length of the output to fit your requirements. Keep in mind that very low max tokens might result in incomplete or truncated sentences.

Example Prompts with Different Max Tokens:

"Summarize the key points of the novel 'To Kill a Mockingbird' by Harper Lee. Max Tokens: 150"

High Max Tokens (e.g., 150):
Expect a more detailed summary that covers major plot points, character arcs, and themes.

"Summarize the key points of the novel 'To Kill a Mockingbird' by Harper Lee. Max Tokens: 50"

Low Max Tokens (e.g., 50):
Expect a concise summary focusing on the most essential elements of the story, possibly omitting some details.

Experimenting with Temperature and Max Tokens

To achieve the optimal balance between creativity and coherence or length and conciseness, experiment with different temperature and max token values for your prompts. Adjusting these parameters allows you to tailor the AI-generated output to your specific needs and preferences.

Remember, the art of Prompt Engineering involves iterative experimentation. Don't be afraid to try various combinations of temperature and max tokens to find the perfect settings for your ChatGPT interactions!

By mastering these two parameters, you'll unlock a whole new level of control and customization, taking your ChatGPT experience to new heights. In the next section, we'll continue our journey into the world of Prompt Engineering, uncovering more advanced techniques to elevate your AI-generated text even further. Stay tuned!

3.3 Using System Messages and User Messages

In this section, we'll explore the use of system messages and user messages, two powerful tools that can help you create dynamic and interactive conversations with ChatGPT. By understanding how to use these message types effectively, you'll be able to guide the AI's responses more precisely and create engaging, multi-turn interactions.

System Messages

System messages are used to provide initial context or instructions to ChatGPT. These messages are an excellent way to set the stage for your conversation or to establish the role the AI should take during the interaction. System messages are processed by the AI before any user messages, ensuring that the AI has the necessary context from the start.

Example System Messages:

[Roleplay Context]:

"You are an AI assistant helping users with their gardening questions."

[Instructional Context]:

"In this conversation, provide detailed information about famous historical events."

User Messages

User messages are the primary means of communication between you and ChatGPT. They allow you to pose questions, provide additional context, or give further instructions during an ongoing conversation. User messages help guide the AI's responses and create a more engaging and interactive experience.

Example User Messages:

[Follow-up Question]:

"What are some common pests that affect tomato plants, and how can I prevent them?"

[Additional Context]:

"I'm growing cherry tomatoes in a small urban garden."

Combining System Messages and User Messages

By skillfully combining system messages and user messages, you can create dynamic conversations that flow naturally and effectively. Use system messages to set the context or role, and then guide the conversation using user messages. This combination allows you to maintain control over the interaction while still benefiting from the AI's capabilities.

Example Conversation with System and User Messages:

[System Message]:

> "You are a knowledgeable nutritionist providing advice on healthy eating habits."

[User Message]:

> "What are some nutrient-dense foods that I can incorporate into my daily diet?"

Some nutrient-dense foods you can include in your daily diet are leafy greens, berries, nuts, seeds, lean proteins, and whole grains. These foods are packed with vitamins, minerals, and other essential nutrients, providing a wide range of health benefits.

As you experiment with system messages and user messages, remember that it's essential to strike a balance between providing enough context and allowing the AI room to generate creative and informative responses. By mastering these message types, you'll be well on your way to creating engaging and interactive conversations with ChatGPT. Happy chatting!

3.4 Beginner Tutorial and Sample Problems

Now that you have a foundational understanding of crafting effective prompts and using system and user messages, let's put those skills to the test! In this beginner tutorial, we'll walk you through a series of sample problems, guiding you step by step in creating prompts and interacting with ChatGPT.

Sample Problem 1: Recipe Ideas

Objective: Generate a list of vegetarian dinner recipes using specific ingredients.

Prompt Crafting:

1. Define your objective: Generate a list of vegetarian dinner recipes.
2. Be specific: Include the ingredients you want to use in your recipes.

Prompt Example:

"Provide a list of five vegetarian dinner recipes that include quinoa, black beans, and bell peppers."

Sample Problem 2: Summary of a Movie

Objective: Summarize the plot of a movie for a friend who hasn't seen it.

Prompt Crafting:

1. Define your objective: Summarize the plot of a movie.

2. Provide context: Include the movie title and relevant details.

Prompt Example:

"Summarize the plot of the movie 'Inception' directed by Christopher Nolan."

Sample Problem 3: Coding Help

Objective: Receive guidance on how to write a simple Python program that calculates the area of a rectangle.

Prompt Crafting:

1. Define your objective: Guidance on writing a Python program.
2. Be specific: Explain the purpose of the program (calculating the area of a rectangle).

Prompt Example:

"Explain how to write a Python program that takes the length and width of a rectangle as inputs and calculates its area."

We've already worked through some sample problems, so let's continue honing your prompt engineering skills with additional examples. These problems will help reinforce the techniques you've learned and build your confidence in interacting with ChatGPT.

Sample Problem 4: Travel Recommendations

Objective: Obtain a list of must-see attractions in Rome, Italy, for a 3-day trip.

Prompt Crafting:

1. Define your objective: Get a list of must-see attractions in Rome.
2. Set constraints: Specify the time frame (3 days).

Prompt Example:

"Provide a list of must-see attractions in Rome, Italy, for a traveler visiting for 3 days."

Sample Problem 5: Creative Writing

Objective: Generate a short story about a detective who solves crimes by traveling back in time.

Prompt Crafting:

1. Define your objective: Write a short story.
2. Be specific: Include the character (detective), the ability (time travel), and the activity (solving crimes).

Prompt Example:

"Write a short story about a detective who solves crimes by traveling back in time."

Sample Problem 6: Debating Pros and Cons

Objective: Learn about the advantages and disadvantages of renewable energy sources.

Prompt Crafting:

1. Define your objective: Discuss the pros and cons of renewable energy.
2. Ask open-ended questions: Encourage the AI to provide detailed information on the topic.

Prompt Example:

"Explain the advantages and disadvantages of using renewable energy sources, such as solar and wind power."

By working through these sample problems, you've practiced crafting effective prompts, setting constraints, and asking open-ended questions. Remember that prompt engineering is an iterative process, so don't hesitate to refine your prompts and experiment with different approaches. As you continue your journey with ChatGPT, you'll become more adept at creating prompts that yield the desired results. Keep practicing, and have fun exploring the limitless possibilities of AI-powered conversation!

CHAPTER 4

INTERMEDIATE TECHNIQUES IN PROMPT ENGINEERING

Congratulations on your progress so far! You've mastered the basics of crafting effective prompts and working with system and user messages. Now it's time to level up your skills with some intermediate techniques in prompt engineering. These strategies will help you take full advantage of ChatGPT's capabilities, enabling you to generate even more precise and targeted responses.

In this chapter, we'll delve deeper into the world of prompt engineering, exploring techniques such as chaining prompts, using conditional statements, and incorporating retrieval and generative modes. We'll also provide more advanced sample problems and tutorials to help you put these newfound skills into practice.

By the end of this chapter, you'll be well-equipped to tackle more complex and nuanced interactions with ChatGPT. Your journey towards mastery continues, so let's dive in and unlock the full potential of this powerful AI companion!

4.1 Building Context and Conversation History

Establishing context and maintaining conversation history is crucial for creating interactive and engaging exchanges with ChatGPT. In this section, we'll discuss how to effectively build context and conversation history to ensure that the AI understands the flow of the conversation and provides accurate and relevant responses.

Building Context

ChatGPT relies heavily on the context provided in a conversation to generate meaningful responses. By building a strong context, you can significantly improve the AI's understanding and ability to respond to your prompts effectively.

Use clear and concise language: Be straightforward with your requests and use language that is easy for the AI to interpret.

Provide necessary details: Supply any relevant information or details that will help the AI understand your request better.

Set constraints: Specify any limitations or guidelines you want the AI to follow while generating a response.

Maintaining Conversation History

Preserving the conversation history is essential for multi-turn conversations, as it allows the AI to refer back to previous exchanges and respond accordingly. Here's how to maintain conversation history effectively:

Include previous messages: When constructing a new prompt, ensure that you include previous user messages and AI-generated responses as part of the conversation history.

Keep track of message order: Maintain the correct order of messages to help the AI understand the flow of the conversation.

Example Prompts:

Example 1: Planning a Trip

"I'm planning a trip to Paris for a week. Can you recommend some must-visit places?"

Certainly! Some must-visit places in Paris include the Eiffel Tower, Louvre Museum, Notre-Dame Cathedral, Montmartre, and the Palace of Versailles.

"Thanks! Can you also suggest some local French restaurants near the Louvre Museum?"

In this example, the conversation history is maintained by including the previous user message and AI-generated response. This helps ChatGPT understand the ongoing discussion and provide relevant restaurant suggestions.

Example 2: Homework Help

"I need help with a math problem. Calculate the derivative of the function $f(x) = x^3 - 4x^2 + 6x - 8$."

The derivative of the function $f(x) = x^3 - 4x^2 + 6x - 8$ is $f'(x) = 3x^2 - 8x + 6$.

"Thanks! Now, can you help me find the critical points of the function?"

In this example, the conversation history is preserved to ensure that ChatGPT knows which function the user is referring to when asking for critical points.

By building context and maintaining conversation history, you'll improve the accuracy and relevance of ChatGPT's responses in multi-turn conversations. Practice these techniques in your interactions with the AI to create seamless and engaging conversational experiences.

4.2 Prompt Chaining and Multi-Step Tasks

Sometimes, you may want to accomplish more complex tasks that require multiple steps or a series of questions and answers. In these cases, prompt chaining can be a valuable technique to guide ChatGPT through multi-step tasks. In this section, we'll explore how to chain prompts effectively and provide examples to demonstrate this powerful strategy.

Prompt Chaining

Prompt chaining involves breaking down a complex task into smaller, more manageable steps and then guiding the AI through these steps using a series of prompts. This technique allows you to maintain control over the conversation and ensures that ChatGPT stays on track while addressing your requests.

To create effective prompt chains:

1. Identify the individual steps: Break down your complex task into a series of smaller tasks or questions.

2. Craft prompts for each step: Write concise and clear prompts for each subtask or question.
3. Chain prompts together: Guide the AI through the process by using the output from one prompt as input for the next.

Example Prompts:

Example 1: Developing a Story Outline

Step 1: "Generate a story idea about a time-traveling detective."

A time-traveling detective named Eliza discovers a mysterious pocket watch that allows her to travel through time and solve cold cases that were never cracked.

Step 2: "Based on the story idea, create a list of three main events that happen in the story."

1. Eliza finds the pocket watch and uncovers its time-traveling abilities.

2. Eliza solves a high-profile cold case from the past, attracting the attention of powerful enemies.

3. Eliza confronts the antagonist and uncovers a hidden connection between them, ultimately deciding the fate of her time-traveling abilities.

Example 2: Multi-Step Math Problem

Step 1:"Find the roots of the quadratic equation 2x^2 - 5x + 3 = 0."

The roots of the equation 2x^2 - 5x + 3 = 0 are x = 1 and x = 1.5."

Step 2: "Now, find the vertex of the parabola represented by the equation 2x^2 - 5x + 3."

The vertex of the parabola represented by the equation 2x^2 - 5x + 3 is (1.25, -0.5).

By practicing prompt chaining and breaking complex tasks into smaller steps, you can effectively guide ChatGPT through multi-step tasks and obtain the desired results. This technique will enhance your ability to interact with the AI and unlock new possibilities for collaboration and problem-solving.

4.3 Refining Output with Prompt Iteration

In some cases, you might receive an output from ChatGPT that is close to what you want but not quite perfect. In these situations, prompt iteration can help you refine the AI's output to better match your requirements. In this section, we'll explore how to iterate on prompts effectively and provide examples to demonstrate this process.

Prompt Iteration

Prompt iteration involves tweaking and adjusting your initial prompt based on the AI's output to guide the AI towards producing a more desirable response. This technique allows you to fine-tune the AI's understanding of your request and obtain more accurate or specific results.

To create effective prompt iterations:

1. Assess the AI's response: Evaluate the AI-generated output to identify areas where it needs improvement or refinement.
2. Modify the prompt: Adjust the wording of your prompt to address any issues or provide additional guidance to the AI.
3. Repeat as necessary: Continue iterating on your prompt until you obtain the desired output.

Example Prompts:

Example 1: Expanding a Story Idea

[Initial Prompt]:

"Generate a story idea about a time-traveling detective."

A time-traveling detective named Eliza discovers a mysterious pocket watch that allows her to travel through time and solve cold cases that were never cracked.

[Iterated Prompt]:

> "Expand on the story idea about a time-traveling detective, including details about her first case and the challenges she faces." AI-generated

Eliza, a skilled detective, stumbles upon a mysterious pocket watch that grants her the power to travel through time. Her first case involves a missing heiress from the 1920s, whose disappearance has remained unsolved for decades. As Eliza delves deeper into the past, she uncovers a web of secrets and deceit, facing challenges that test her skills as a detective and force her to confront the ethical implications of her newfound abilities."

Example 2: Clarifying a Math Solution

[Initial Prompt]:

> "Solve the equation $2x + 3 = 5x - 2$." AI-generated

The solution to the equation $2x + 3 = 5x - 2$ is $x = 1$.

[Iterated Prompt]:

> "Please provide a step-by-step solution for the equation 2x + 3 = 5x - 2."

To solve the equation 2x + 3 = 5x - 2, follow these steps:

Step 1: Subtract 2x from both sides of the equation: 3 = 3x - 2

Step 2: Add 2 to both sides of the equation: 5 = 3x

Step 3: Divide both sides by 3: x = 5/3

By iterating on your prompts and refining them based on the AI's output, you can guide ChatGPT towards producing more accurate and tailored responses. This technique will help you get the most out of your interactions with the AI and ensure that it meets your specific needs and requirements.

4.4 Intermediate Tutorial and Sample Problems

Now that we've covered various intermediate techniques in prompt engineering, it's time to put your newfound knowledge into practice. In this section, we'll provide a tutorial and several sample problems that challenge you to use the strategies we've discussed. Remember to include context, prompt chaining, and prompt iteration as you work through these problems.

Tutorial: Writing a Short Story Using Prompt Chaining

Your goal is to create a short story using prompt chaining. Start by generating a story idea, then use a series of prompts to develop characters, setting, and plot. Finally, iterate on your prompts to refine the story.

Step 1: Generate a story idea:

> "Generate a story idea about an astronaut stranded on an alien planet."

An astronaut named Alex finds himself stranded on an alien planet after his spacecraft crash-lands. He discovers that the planet is inhabited by an intelligent alien species, and he must learn to communicate and cooperate with them to survive and find a way back home.

Step 2: Develop characters:

> "Describe the main character Alex and two important alien characters he meets on the alien planet."

Alex is a resourceful and determined astronaut with a background in engineering. Despite the challenges he faces, he remains optimistic and open-minded. On the alien planet, he encounters Zara, a wise and empathetic alien scientist who is intrigued by humans and eager to learn from them. He also meets Tark, a skeptical and cautious alien leader who is initially distrustful of Alex but comes to see him as an ally over time."

Step 3: Develop setting:

"Describe the environment and society of the alien planet."

"The alien planet is a lush, vibrant world filled with unique flora and fauna. The atmosphere is breathable for humans, but the weather is unpredictable, with frequent storms and drastic temperature fluctuations. The alien society is highly advanced, with technology that surpasses that of Earth. Their social structure is based on cooperation and the pursuit of knowledge, with an emphasis on harmony between their species and their environment."

Step 4: Develop plot:

"Outline a plot for the story, including the climax and resolution."

As Alex works with Zara and Tark to repair his spacecraft, he learns more about the alien culture and forms a strong bond with them. The climax occurs when a natural disaster threatens the alien civilization, and Alex must use his engineering skills to help them. Through their combined efforts, they avert disaster and prove the value of cooperation between species. In the end, Alex's spacecraft is repaired, and he returns to Earth with newfound appreciation for the diverse universe and the friendships he

Sample Problems

1. Craft a series of prompts to research and write a 500-word article about the impact of climate change on polar bears. Consider the following aspects: habitat loss, food sources, and conservation efforts.
2. Develop a series of prompts to create a lesson plan for teaching high school students about the American Civil War. Include objectives, key concepts, activities, and assessment methods.
3. Use prompt chaining to plan a surprise birthday party for a friend. Consider the following aspects: theme, guest list, location, food, and entertainment.

Remember, as you work through these problems, don't hesitate to iterate on your prompts and refine them based on the AI's output. With practice, you'll develop a deeper understanding of how to make the most of ChatGPT's capabilities.

We hope this chapter has provided you with valuable insights into intermediate prompt engineering techniques. As you move forward, you'll be able to tackle more complex tasks and collaborate more effectively with ChatGPT.

ADVANCED TECHNIQUES IN PROMPT ENGINEERING

Welcome to Chapter 5, where we'll dive into advanced techniques in prompt engineering that will truly elevate your expertise in using ChatGPT. By now, you have a solid foundation in crafting effective prompts, experimenting with temperature and max tokens, building context and conversation history, and refining your output through iteration. As you venture into advanced strategies, you'll unlock even more potential in your AI interactions.

In this chapter, we'll explore advanced prompt engineering techniques, such as Manipulating output with Tokens and Pattern Matching, guiding Chatgpt's responses with reinforcement learning and combining multiple APIs and external data sources. Like we've done in previously we wrap up this chapter by exploring and implementing advanced tutorials and sample problems.

By mastering these advanced techniques, you'll be well-equipped to tackle a wide range of tasks and challenges, making the most of ChatGPT's capabilities. So, buckle up and get ready for a deep dive into the world of advanced prompt engineering!

5.1 Manipulating Output with Tokens and Pattern Matching

Get ready for some fun, because we're about to explore the art of manipulating output with tokens and pattern matching! These techniques will help you fine-tune ChatGPT's responses, giving you more control over the content and style of the generated text.

Tokens and Pattern Matching: A Dynamic Duo

Tokens are the building blocks of text in ChatGPT. A token can be as short as one character or as long as one word, and understanding how tokens work can help you tailor your prompts for optimal results.

Pattern matching, on the other hand, involves identifying and manipulating specific patterns in the AI's responses. By combining tokens and pattern matching, you'll have a powerful set of tools to create custom-tailored output.

Token Manipulation: The Building Blocks

To manipulate tokens, you can experiment with the **max_tokens** parameter. By setting a specific number, you'll limit the response length, forcing ChatGPT to generate shorter or longer responses based on your requirements.

Example:

> "What are the three main benefits of exercise?" Max tokens: 10"

1. Improved mood. 2. Increased energy. 3. Better sleep.

Pattern Matching: Guiding the Output

To use pattern matching, you can structure your prompt in a way that encourages the AI to generate responses following a specific pattern.

Example:

[Prompt]:

> "List 5 types of fruit and their primary nutrients, formatted
> as: [fruit] - [nutrient]."

1. Apple - Vitamin C. 2. Banana - Potassium. 3. Blueberries -
Antioxidants. 4. Kiwi - Vitamin K. 5. Orange - Vitamin C.

Combining Tokens and Pattern Matching

To achieve even greater control, you can combine token
manipulation and pattern matching in your prompts.

Example:

[Prompt]:

> "Write a 10-word summary of the benefits of yoga." Max
> tokens: 10

"Increases flexibility, strength, balance; promotes relaxation,
focus, and stress relief."

Practice Makes Perfect

It's time to flex your newfound skills! Try these sample
problems to put token manipulation and pattern matching to
the test:

1. Create a prompt that generates a 6-word slogan for a
   fictional environmental organization.

2. Request a list of 7 outdoor activities, formatted as: "[activity] - [primary benefit]."
3. Design a prompt that produces a concise 15-word description of your favorite hobby.

Remember, practice makes perfect! The more you experiment with tokens and pattern matching, the better you'll become at crafting effective prompts that yield the desired output. So, keep up the good work, and let's continue our journey into the advanced techniques of prompt engineering!

5.2 Guiding AI Response with Reinforcement Learning

Hold on to your hats, because we're diving into the fascinating world of reinforcement learning! By guiding AI responses using this powerful technique, you'll be able to train ChatGPT to produce outputs that are even better suited to your specific needs.

What is Reinforcement Learning?

Reinforcement learning is a type of machine learning where an AI agent learns to make decisions by receiving feedback in the form of rewards or penalties. In the context of ChatGPT, this means adjusting the model's behavior based on user feedback to improve its performance.

InstructGPT: A Step Forward

OpenAI introduced InstructGPT, a model trained using reinforcement learning from human feedback (RLHF). This technique allows ChatGPT to better follow instructions and provide more accurate and relevant responses. By incorporating reinforcement learning, the AI becomes a more effective tool for users.

Using Reinforcement Learning with ChatGPT

While you can't directly apply reinforcement learning to your ChatGPT interactions, you can leverage the power of InstructGPT by carefully crafting your prompts to provide clear instructions and desired outcomes.

Example 1:

[Vague prompt]:

> "Tell me something about dogs."

[Instructive prompt]:

> "Provide three interesting facts about the history of dog domestication."

By making your prompt more instructive, you can guide the AI toward generating a response that meets your specific requirements.

Example 2:

[Vague prompt]:

> "Write a story."

[Instructive Prompt]:

> "Write a short story about a young wizard on her first day at a magical academy."

Adding context and clear instructions helps the AI understand the type of story you want, resulting in a more focused and engaging output.

Sample Prompts for Practice

Now, let's put your instructive prompt-crafting skills to the test! Try creating instructive prompts for the following scenarios:

1. Obtaining a detailed overview of the benefits of a plant-based diet.
2. Receiving advice on how to improve your public speaking skills.
3. Gathering information about the history and cultural significance of a famous landmark.

Remember, the key to guiding AI responses is providing clear instructions and specifying the desired outcomes. By practicing this skill, you'll be able to harness the full potential of ChatGPT and make the most of your AI interactions. Keep up the great work, and let's continue exploring advanced techniques in prompt engineering!

5.3 Combining Multiple APIs and External Data Sources

Get ready to level up your ChatGPT skills even further, because we're about to explore the exciting realm of combining multiple APIs and external data sources! By integrating additional tools and information into your ChatGPT interactions, you'll create even more powerful and versatile applications.

Why Combine APIs and External Data Sources?

While ChatGPT is an incredibly powerful language model, it may not always have the most up-to-date or specialized information to suit your needs. By combining it with other APIs and external data sources, you can enhance its capabilities and provide more accurate, relevant, and personalized responses.

How to Combine APIs and External Data Sources

To combine multiple APIs or external data sources with ChatGPT, you'll generally follow these steps:

1. Choose the appropriate APIs or data sources that complement ChatGPT's abilities.
2. Retrieve data from the chosen sources using their respective APIs or methods.
3. Process and format the data as needed.
4. Incorporate the data into your ChatGPT prompt, providing context and instructions for the AI to utilize the information effectively.

Example: Weather Forecasting

Imagine you want to create an application that provides personalized weather forecasts. You could combine ChatGPT with a weather API to generate a user-friendly, informative forecast.

1. Choose a reliable weather API, such as OpenWeatherMap or Weather API.
2. Retrieve the weather data for the user's location.
3. Process and format the data into an easily readable format.
4. Craft a prompt that instructs ChatGPT to generate a personalized forecast based on the retrieved data.

[Example prompt]:

> "Generate a personalized weather forecast for a user in San Francisco with the following weather data: {formatted_weather_data}"

Example: Stock Market Insights

Let's say you want to build a financial application that provides insights into stock market trends. You could combine ChatGPT with a financial API like Alpha Vantage or Quandl to generate valuable stock market analysis.

1. Choose a suitable financial API.
2. Retrieve relevant stock market data.
3. Process and format the data as needed.
4. Create a prompt that instructs ChatGPT to analyze the stock market data and provide insights.

[Example prompt]:

"Analyze the following stock market data and provide a brief summary of the current trends and potential investment opportunities: {formatted_stock_data}"

Practice Scenarios

It's time to flex your creative muscles and practice combining ChatGPT with other APIs and external data sources. Try devising your own applications using the following concepts:

1. A travel planner that combines ChatGPT with a flight booking API and hotel booking API.
2. A language learning tool that utilizes ChatGPT and a translation API.
3. A personalized exercise planner that integrates ChatGPT with a fitness API.

By combining multiple APIs and external data sources with ChatGPT, you'll unlock a world of possibilities and create powerful applications that cater to various needs. Keep up the fantastic work, and let's continue to hone your expertise in prompt engineering!

5.4 Advanced Tutorial and Sample Problems

Congratulations on making it this far! In this final section of Chapter 5, we'll put your advanced prompt engineering skills to the test with a hands-on tutorial and a series of challenging sample problems. Don't worry; you've got this! And remember, after this section, we'll dive into Chapter 6, where we'll explore the limitations and biases of ChatGPT, helping you become a well-rounded AI expert.

Advanced Tutorial: Collaborative Story Writing

For this tutorial, let's create a ChatGPT-powered collaborative story-writing system. You'll start a story, and then ChatGPT will take turns with you, generating the next paragraph based on the provided story context.

1. Begin by writing the first paragraph of a story. Be creative and set the scene for an engaging narrative.
2. Craft a prompt for Chatgpt that includes the story so far and clear instructions to continue the narrative. For example:
   "Continue the following story by adding the next paragraph: {your_story_paragraph}"
3. Take turns with ChatGPT, building on each other's paragraphs, and watch your collaborative story unfold!

Sample Problems

Now that you've explored the possibilities of advanced prompt engineering with the tutorial, try your hand at these sample problems that further test your skills:

1. Create a ChatGPT-powered system that generates personalized workout plans. Craft a prompt that instructs ChatGPT to provide a week-long workout plan for a user with specific fitness goals and preferences.
2. Design a ChatGPT-based financial advisor that helps users create monthly budget plans. Retrieve information about the user's income, expenses, and financial goals, and craft a prompt that instructs ChatGPT to provide a personalized budget plan.

3. Develop a ChatGPT-powered study guide that combines data from a subject-specific API, like a math or history API, with ChatGPT's natural language understanding. Retrieve information about a specific topic and craft a prompt that instructs ChatGPT to provide a concise and informative study guide.

You've done an incredible job mastering advanced prompt engineering techniques! As we move on to Chapter 6: Understanding Limitations and Biases of ChatGPT, we'll take a closer look at the inherent limitations and biases of AI systems like ChatGPT. By understanding these factors, you'll be better equipped to utilize ChatGPT effectively and responsibly. So, let's keep the momentum going and dive right in!

CHAPTER 6

UNDERSTANDING LIMITATIONS AND BIASES OF CHATGPT

Welcome to Chapter 6, where we'll venture beyond the world of prompt engineering and delve into the often-overlooked aspects of working with AI systems like ChatGPT. As powerful and versatile as ChatGPT may be, it's essential to recognize and understand its limitations and biases to use it effectively and responsibly.

In this chapter, we'll dissect the inherent limitations in AI-generated text, address the biases and ethical considerations associated with using ChatGPT, and provide you with best practices for mitigating these limitations and biases. By the end of this chapter, you'll not only be a ChatGPT expert but also an informed and responsible AI practitioner.

So, let's dive in and explore the less glamorous, yet equally important side of ChatGPT, so that you can harness its power without falling prey to its pitfalls!

6.1 Inherent Limitations in AI-generated Text

As much as we love the magic of ChatGPT, it's important to acknowledge that it isn't perfect. In this section, we'll explore some of the inherent limitations in AI-generated text and provide examples to help you recognize and navigate these limitations effectively.

Lengthy Responses

One common limitation is that ChatGPT may produce verbose responses when a short, concise answer would be more appropriate. For example, when asking:

"What is the capital of France?"

A desired response might be: "Paris."

However, ChatGPT might generate a more verbose response like:

The capital of France is the beautiful and historic city of Paris, known for its iconic landmarks, rich culture, and exquisite cuisine."

To address this limitation, you can refine your prompt by explicitly asking for a concise response:

"Give me a one-word answer: What is the capital of France?"

Lack of Source Attribution

Another limitation is that ChatGPT may provide information without citing its sources, making it difficult to verify the accuracy of the response. For example, when asking:

"Who invented the telephone?"

ChatGPT might respond with:

"The telephone was invented by Alexander Graham Bell."

To address this limitation, you can refine your prompt by requesting source attribution:

"Who invented the telephone? Please provide a source for your answer."

Misunderstandings

ChatGPT may sometimes misunderstand the context or intent behind a prompt, leading to irrelevant or incorrect responses. For example, when asking:

> "Who won the 2022 World Series?"

If ChatGPT responds with:

The 2022 World Series was won by the Chicago Bulls.

it has clearly misunderstood the context since the Chicago Bulls are a basketball team.

To address this limitation, you can refine your prompt by providing additional context or constraints:

> "Who won the 2022 World Series in Major League Baseball?"

Plausible but Incorrect Answers

ChatGPT may sometimes generate plausible-sounding but incorrect answers. This is often due to the model relying on patterns it has learned from the training data, which may not always be accurate or up-to-date. For example, when asking:

> "Who is the current CEO of Apple?"

If ChatGPT responds with:

The current CEO of Apple is Tim Cook

this answer may be outdated if there has been a recent change in leadership.

To address this limitation, it's important to verify information provided by ChatGPT, especially when it pertains to time-sensitive or critical data.

These are just a few examples of the inherent limitations in AI-generated text. By being aware of these limitations and refining your prompts, you can work around them to achieve more accurate and relevant responses from ChatGPT. In the next section, we'll discuss biases and ethical considerations, shedding light on another critical aspect of working with AI systems like ChatGPT.

6.2 Addressing Biases and Ethical Considerations

AI systems like ChatGPT are trained on vast amounts of data from the internet, which exposes them to the risk of learning and reproducing biases present in those data sources. In this section, we'll discuss how biases can manifest in AI-generated text and explore ethical considerations to be aware of when using ChatGPT.

Biases in AI-generated Text

Biases can emerge in a variety of ways, including stereotypes, underrepresentation, or overrepresentation of certain groups. For example, if you ask ChatGPT:

> "Who are some famous computer scientists?"

It might respond with a list that predominantly features male scientists, inadvertently perpetuating a gender bias in the field of computer science.

Ethical Considerations

Understanding and addressing the biases in AI-generated text is crucial to ensure that we use AI systems like ChatGPT responsibly and ethically. As an AI practitioner, you must be aware of the potential biases in the outputs generated by AI models and strive to mitigate them.

Here are some steps you can take to address biases and ethical considerations when using ChatGPT:

1. **Acknowledge and Understand**: Recognize that biases can exist in AI-generated text, and educate yourself on the types of biases that might emerge in different contexts.

2. **Test and Iterate**: Test your prompts and responses for potential biases by trying various inputs and observing the outputs. If you notice biases, refine your prompts or use techniques discussed in previous chapters to guide the AI towards more balanced and accurate responses.

3. **Be Transparent**: Inform your users that your application uses AI and that the outputs may contain biases. Encourage users to provide feedback on any biases they encounter, which can help you improve the system and make it more inclusive.

4. **Stay Updated**: Keep track of advancements in AI research and industry best practices on mitigating biases. Adopt new techniques and tools as they become available to ensure

that your use of AI systems like ChatGPT remains ethical and responsible.

By taking these steps, you can help create a more inclusive and fair AI experience for all users. In the next section, we'll discuss best practices for mitigating limitations and biases, arming you with the knowledge you need to make the most of ChatGPT while being mindful of its potential pitfalls.

6.3 Best Practices for Mitigating Limitations and Biases

Being aware of the limitations and biases of ChatGPT is the first step towards addressing them. In this section, we'll outline some best practices for mitigating these issues and ensuring that your use of ChatGPT is responsible and ethical.

Mitigating Limitations

Iterative Prompting: If ChatGPT doesn't provide the desired output in the first attempt, try rephrasing the question, providing more context, or using other prompt engineering techniques discussed in previous chapters.

Fact-Checking: Since ChatGPT might sometimes generate plausible-sounding but incorrect or outdated information, always verify the facts and data it provides, especially for critical applications.

Set Boundaries: If ChatGPT tends to generate content that is too verbose or irrelevant, experiment with temperature and max tokens settings to better control the output.

Mitigating Biases

Diversify Inputs: Use diverse inputs and question formulations to explore different perspectives and uncover potential biases in AI-generated text.

Monitor Outputs: Regularly review the outputs generated by ChatGPT to identify and address any biases or inaccuracies. Encourage users to provide feedback if they notice any issues.

Inclusive Language: When crafting prompts, strive to use inclusive language that avoids stereotypes and promotes a fair representation of different groups.

As you become more adept at identifying and addressing limitations and biases, your use of ChatGPT will become more responsible and effective. With this newfound understanding, you're now ready to dive into the exciting world of ChatGPT use cases!

In Chapter 7: ChatGPT Use Cases, we'll explore various applications for ChatGPT, from translations and summarizing to learning to code and monetizing ChatGPT applications. You'll discover how this powerful AI tool can enhance your creativity, productivity, and problem-solving skills across a wide range of domains.

CHAPTER 7

CHATGPT USE CASES - UNLOCK THE POWER OF CHATGPT

Congratulations on reaching Chapter 7! By now, you've gained a strong understanding of ChatGPT, from the basics to advanced prompt engineering techniques. You're well-equipped to tackle the world of AI-assisted tasks with confidence. But you may be wondering, "How can I apply these skills in real-life situations?" Well, you're in for a treat!

In this chapter, we'll delve into a wide array of practical use cases for ChatGPT. From brainstorming ideas and translations to learning to code and monetizing applications, you'll discover the versatility and power of this AI tool. Each section will cover techniques, tips, and strategies specific to that use case, accompanied by tutorials and sample problems to help you build your expertise.

Whether you're a writer, student, professional, or just a curious individual, this chapter is your launchpad to harnessing the full potential of ChatGPT. Let's dive into the exciting world of ChatGPT use cases and unlock your creativity, productivity, and problem-solving prowess!

7.1 Brainstorming ideas

Welcome to the wondrous world of brainstorming with ChatGPT! This fantastic AI buddy of yours is an idea-generating machine that can help you unlock your creative potential like never before. In this section, we'll explore the techniques to make the most of ChatGPT's brainstorming prowess, and we'll provide example prompts for you to practice your skills. Ready to be blown away by a whirlwind of inspiration? Let's get started!

Techniques for effective brainstorming with ChatGPT

Open-ended questions: Start by asking ChatGPT open-ended questions to kick off your brainstorming session. Questions like "What are some creative ways to...?" or "How can we improve...?" help set the stage for a fruitful idea-generating conversation.

[Example prompt]:

> "What are some innovative ideas for promoting an eco-friendly lifestyle?"

Encourage lateral thinking: To get ChatGPT to think outside the box, try asking for unconventional or unexpected ideas. Phrases like "surprising," "unusual," or "uncommon" can be helpful to guide the AI towards more novel suggestions.

[Example prompt]:

> "What are some unusual marketing strategies for a new restaurant?"

Narrow down your focus: Sometimes, it's helpful to narrow down your focus to a specific area. You can do this by adding context or constraints to your prompts.

[Example prompt]:

> "What are some creative ways to use technology in the classroom for better student engagement?"

Combine ideas: Leverage ChatGPT's ability to combine multiple ideas or concepts by asking it to generate ideas that merge different elements.

[Example prompt]:

> "How can we combine the concepts of gamification and fitness to create a unique workout experience?"

Iterate and refine: Don't hesitate to iterate and refine your prompts. If ChatGPT provides an interesting idea but you want to explore it further or tweak it, simply adjust your prompt and continue the brainstorming process.

[Example prompt]:

> "You mentioned using virtual reality for immersive workouts. What are some specific applications or examples of how this could work?"

Tutorial and sample problems

Now it's time to put your brainstorming skills to the test! Try your hand at the following sample problems and see what innovative ideas ChatGPT comes up with.

Sample problem 1: Brainstorm ideas for an unconventional travel app that caters to adventure seekers.

[Suggested prompt]:

> "What are some unique features or functionalities for a travel app aimed at adventure seekers?"

Sample problem 2: Generate marketing ideas for a new board game targeted at families.

[Suggested prompt]:

"What are some fun and engaging marketing strategies for a family-oriented board game?"

Sample problem 3: Come up with ways to repurpose an old, unused factory building.

[Suggested prompt]:

"What are some creative ways to transform an abandoned factory into a useful and attractive space?"

Remember, the sky's the limit when brainstorming with ChatGPT. So let your imagination run wild, and don't be afraid to experiment with different techniques and approaches. Happy brainstorming!

7.2 Translations

Hola, amigos! Welcome to the world of translations with ChatGPT. Imagine a language barrier no longer standing in your way, whether you're traveling, making friends from around the globe, or expanding your business internationally. In this section, we'll explore ChatGPT's impressive language support and translation capabilities, specifically focusing on Spanish to English translations and vice versa. So grab your virtual passport, and let's embark on this linguistic adventure together! Remember, our journey will be sprinkled with humor, positivity, and encouragement to make learning and experimenting with translations as delightful as possible. ¡Vamos!

Language support and translation capabilities

ChatGPT boasts an extensive range of language support, making it a powerful tool for translation tasks. While we'll primarily focus on Spanish to English translations (and vice versa) in this section, it's worth noting that ChatGPT can work with many other languages too.

Here's how to make ChatGPT your personal language assistant:

Be explicit: Clearly state the desired language for translation in your prompt. This will ensure that ChatGPT understands the task at hand and provides the most accurate translation.

Example:

[Prompt]:

> "Translate the following English text to Spanish: 'Hello, how are you?'"

 👍 👎

Hola, ¿cómo estás?

Use conversation history: When translating multiple sentences or paragraphs, provide the conversation history to maintain context and improve translation quality.

Example:

> "Translate the following English text to Spanish: 'Once upon a time, in a faraway land, there lived a king and a queen.'"

Había una vez, en una tierra lejana, vivía un rey y una reina.

> "Translate the next sentence: 'They had a beautiful daughter named Princess Isabella.'" ChatGPT: "Tenían una hermosa hija llamada Princesa Isabella."

Experiment with temperature and max tokens: Adjust these parameters to fine-tune the translation output. Higher temperature values may result in more creative translations, while lower values yield more conservative translations. Limiting max tokens can help keep translations concise.

Tutorial and sample problems

Now, let's put your newfound translation skills to the test!

Problem 1: Translate the following English text to Spanish: "The weather is beautiful today."

Solution:

[Prompt]:

> "Translate the following English text to Spanish: 'The weather is beautiful today.'"

El tiempo está hermoso hoy."

Problem 2: Translate the following Spanish text to English: "La comida estaba deliciosa."

Solution:

[Prompt]:

> "Translate the following Spanish text to English: 'La comida estaba deliciosa.'"

The food was delicious.

Ready for more linguistic challenges? Continue exploring ChatGPT's translation capabilities on your own or with friends. The more you practice, the more you'll discover the fantastic world of translations. ¡Buena suerte!

7.3 Summarizing

Welcome to the world of summarizing, where less is more, and brevity is the name of the game! ChatGPT has an uncanny ability to condense large amounts of information into easily digestible chunks, making it your perfect partner for summarizing articles, reports, books, and more. In this section, we'll explore techniques for generating accurate summaries with ChatGPT, followed by some nifty tutorial and sample problems to sharpen your summarizing skills. So, buckle up and get ready to make sense of a sea of information, one succinct summary at a time!

Techniques for generating accurate summaries

Generating accurate summaries with ChatGPT is as much an art as it is a science. Here are some techniques to help you create concise yet comprehensive summaries using ChatGPT:

Be specific with your prompt: Start by clearly defining the task for ChatGPT. For example, instead of asking it to "summarize this article," ask it to "provide a 3-sentence summary of the key points in this article." This will help guide the AI in delivering the desired output.

[Example prompt]:

> "Summarize the following article in 3 sentences, highlighting the main points."

Specify the type of summary: Different situations call for different types of summaries. You can guide ChatGPT to create an informative summary, an executive summary, or an abstract, depending on your needs. Clearly indicate the type of summary you're looking for in your prompt.

[Example prompt]:

> "Create an executive summary of this report, focusing on the most important findings and recommendations."

Break down complex content: When dealing with intricate subjects or long documents, it may be helpful to break the content into smaller sections and ask ChatGPT to summarize each part separately. You can then combine these mini-summaries into a coherent whole.

[Example prompt]:

> "Provide a brief summary of each chapter in this book. Start with Chapter 1: [Chapter Title]."

Iterate and refine: If the initial summary doesn't quite hit the mark, don't be afraid to ask ChatGPT to refine its output. You can request a revision or provide additional guidance to help it generate a more accurate summary.

[Example prompt]:

> "The previous summary was a bit too general. Can you provide a more detailed summary, focusing on the main arguments and supporting evidence?"

Leverage user messages: Utilize user messages to make your instructions more conversational and to guide the AI throughout the summarization process. This can be particularly useful when refining summaries or addressing any issues in the initial output.

[Example prompt]:

> "Provide a 5-sentence summary of this scientific paper, emphasizing the research question, methodology, results, and conclusion."

Now that you've got a handle on these techniques, it's time to put them to the test with some tutorial and sample problems in section 7.3.2. Happy summarizing!

Tutorial and Sample Problems

Now that you're equipped with techniques for generating accurate summaries, let's dive into some fun tutorial and sample problems! Put on your summarizing hat, and let's get started.

Tutorial:

1. Choose an article, blog post, or any other piece of text you'd like to summarize.
2. Craft a prompt using the techniques discussed in section 7.3.1. Remember to be specific with your instructions, specify the type of summary, and use user messages when necessary.
3. Input your prompt into ChatGPT and review the generated summary.
4. If the summary doesn't meet your expectations, iterate and refine by providing additional guidance or asking for revisions.
5. Once you're satisfied with the summary, make a note of the prompt that led to the desired output, and use it as a reference for future summarization tasks.

Sample Problems:

1. Summarize a news article: [Prompt]: "Please provide a 4-sentence summary of this news article, focusing on the key events and main takeaways."

2. Summarize a movie plot: [Prompt]: "Summarize the plot of the movie [Movie Title] in 5 sentences, covering the main characters, conflicts, and resolution."
3. Summarize a research paper: [Prompt]: "Create a concise abstract for this research paper, including the research question, methodology, results, and implications of the findings."
4. Summarize a podcast episode: [Prompt]: "Provide a 3-sentence summary of this podcast episode, highlighting the main topics discussed and any key insights shared by the guests."
5. Summarize a book: [Prompt]: "Create a brief synopsis of the book [Book Title], covering the primary themes, characters, and overall narrative arc."

As you work through these sample problems, remember that practice makes perfect. Keep experimenting, iterating, and refining your prompts to get better at generating accurate summaries with ChatGPT. Happy summarizing, and don't forget to have some fun along the way!

7.4 Writing Articles, Blogs, and Books

Welcome, dear wordsmiths, to the exciting world of writing articles, blogs, and books with the help of ChatGPT! In this section, we'll explore how our AI companion can assist you in crafting engaging and captivating content, from the first spark of an idea to the final polished piece. By the end of this journey, you'll be weaving words like a pro, with ChatGPT by your side as your trusty writing sidekick. So, grab your favorite writing instrument (or keyboard, let's be honest), and let's dive into the creative and delightful process of writing with ChatGPT!

Tips for Creating Engaging Content with ChatGPT

Are you ready to dive into the world of content creation with ChatGPT as your trusty sidekick? Here are some tips and tricks to help you make the most of your AI-powered collaboration and produce content that captivates your audience.

Define your purpose: Start by identifying the objective of your piece. Are you writing to inform, entertain, persuade, or inspire? Knowing your goal will help you guide ChatGPT in crafting content that aligns with your vision.

[Example prompt]:

> "Assist me in writing an informative yet engaging article about the history of bicycles."

Establish context: Provide ChatGPT with a clear context, including the target audience, tone, and style you want to convey in your piece. This information helps the AI understand your expectations and create content that meets your requirements.

[Example prompt]:

> "Write an introductory paragraph for a beginner-friendly guide to cryptocurrency trading, using a conversational tone."

Brainstorm creatively: Stuck for ideas? ChatGPT can be your creative brainstorming buddy! Ask for suggestions, like headlines, plot ideas, or even quirky facts, to spark your imagination and get your project moving.

[Example prompt]:

> "Generate 10 fun and engaging article titles related to sustainable living."

Divide and conquer: Tackling a long piece? Break it down into smaller sections or subtopics, and work on them with ChatGPT one by one. This approach not only makes the task more manageable but also helps maintain a logical flow in your content.

[Example prompt]:

> "Help me write a section of an ultimate guide to gardening, focusing on choosing the right plants for your climate."

Ask for multiple angles: Don't settle for the first response from ChatGPT. Experiment with different perspectives, additional details, or alternative takes to find the perfect fit for your content.

[Example prompt]:

> "Write a short paragraph about the benefits of using solar energy, emphasizing environmental impact. Then, write another paragraph focusing on the cost savings."

Revise and refine: ChatGPT might not always hit the bullseye on the first try. Feel free to rephrase your prompts, ask for elaboration, or request rewrites to hone your content to perfection.

[Example prompt]:

> "Revise the previous paragraph about solar energy benefits, making it more engaging by adding a personal anecdote."

Edit and polish: Once you have a draft, it's time to put on your editor's hat. Review the text for clarity, coherence, and readability, making any necessary adjustments to ensure your content shines. Keep in mind that ChatGPT is here to help you in the writing process, but it's ultimately up to you to add the final polish.

Armed with these tips, you're ready to explore the exciting world of content creation alongside ChatGPT. So, buckle up, and let the creative journey begin!

Tutorial and Sample Problems

Ready to put those tips into action and create some stellar content with ChatGPT? This tutorial will walk you through a step-by-step process, complete with sample problems, to help you make the most of your AI-powered writing experience.

Tutorial

Step 1: Define your topic and purpose Choose a topic you're passionate about and decide on the purpose of your content. Remember, you can write to inform, entertain, persuade, or inspire.

[Example prompt]:

> "I want to write an entertaining blog post about the most bizarre ice cream flavors from around the world."

Step 2: Establish context and tone Clarify the target audience, tone, and style you want to convey in your piece. This helps ChatGPT understand your expectations and tailor its output accordingly.

[Example prompt]:

> "Help me write an introductory paragraph for a light-hearted and entertaining blog post about bizarre ice cream flavors, targeting a young adult audience."

Step 3: Brainstorm creatively Ask ChatGPT to generate ideas or suggestions related to your topic. This could be a list of flavors, fun facts, or even anecdotes to include in your post.

[Example prompt]:

> "List 10 bizarre ice cream flavors from around the world, along with a brief description of each."

Step 4: Organize your content Outline the structure of your blog post, dividing it into sections or subtopics. This will help you maintain a logical flow and ensure your piece is easy to follow.

[Example prompt]:

> "Help me create an outline for a blog post about bizarre ice cream flavors, including an introduction, 5 main sections for different flavors, and a conclusion."

Step 5: Write, refine, and revise Work with ChatGPT to develop each section of your blog post. Remember to ask for multiple angles, additional details, or alternative takes to find the perfect fit.

[Example prompt]:

> "Write a fun and engaging paragraph about the lobster ice cream flavor, including its origin and a brief taste description."

Step 6: Edit and polish Once you have a complete draft, review it for clarity, coherence, and readability. Make any necessary adjustments and don't hesitate to ask ChatGPT for assistance in refining your content.

[Example prompt]:

> "Help me rewrite the conclusion of my blog post to leave readers craving more bizarre ice cream flavors."

Sample Problems

Now that you've completed the tutorial, try your hand at these sample problems to practice your newfound skills in content creation with ChatGPT.

1. Write a persuasive paragraph convincing readers to adopt a plant-based diet.
2. Craft a compelling introduction for a blog post about the benefits of meditation.
3. Generate a list of 8 creative topics for a podcast about technology and innovation.
4. Create an outline for a how-to article on building a successful online business.
5. Write a descriptive paragraph about a fictional, magical forest for a fantasy novel.

Remember, practice makes perfect! The more you experiment with ChatGPT, the better you'll become at creating engaging, informative, and entertaining content. So, let your imagination run wild, and happy writing!

7.5 Academic Writing

Fear not, scholarly scribes! ChatGPT is here to assist you in conquering the realm of academic writing. With a little guidance, you'll be able to harness the power of AI to enhance your research papers, reports, and other academic projects. In this section, we'll explore the wonders of adapting ChatGPT to suit your scholarly needs, ensuring that your work is well-researched, structured, and presented in a professional manner. Grab your thinking caps and get ready to dive into the world of academic writing, where ChatGPT will be your trusty sidekick!

Adapting ChatGPT for Research Papers and Reports

When it comes to academic writing, there's no room for error. ChatGPT can be a powerful ally in your quest for scholarly success, but it's essential to guide the AI carefully to ensure accurate and well-structured content. Here are some tips and example prompts to help you adapt ChatGPT for research papers and reports:

Be specific with your prompts: Academic writing requires precision and attention to detail. Make your prompts as specific as possible to get the most relevant information from ChatGPT.

[Example prompt]:

> "Please provide a brief overview of the factors that contribute to climate change and the impact of greenhouse gases on global temperatures."

Request citations and sources: When asking ChatGPT to provide information or research, request citations or sources to back up the content. This will help you verify the information and ensure that it's accurate and up-to-date.

[Example prompt]:

> "What are the main sources of air pollution in urban areas? Please provide at least three examples along with citations from reputable sources."

Organize your content: Academic writing typically follows a structured format. Guide ChatGPT to generate content in a specific order or structure by providing clear instructions.

[Example prompt]:

> "Outline the main sections of a research paper discussing the effects of social media on mental health, including an introduction, literature review, methodology, results, discussion, and conclusion."

Request formal language: Academic writing has a distinct tone and style. Instruct ChatGPT to use formal language and avoid colloquialisms or slang.

[Example prompt]:

> "In formal language, explain the process of photosynthesis and its importance for the survival of plants and the ecosystem."

Proofread and edit: While ChatGPT can generate impressive content, it's important to double-check the output for accuracy, clarity, and consistency. Take the time to proofread and edit the generated text to ensure that it meets academic standards.

Remember, practice makes perfect! Experiment with different prompts and techniques to find the best approach for your academic writing needs. By following these tips and refining your skills, you'll be able to use ChatGPT as an invaluable tool in your scholarly endeavors. Happy researching!

Tutorial and Sample Problems

Ready to put your newfound academic writing skills with ChatGPT to the test? Let's dive into some tutorial exercises and sample problems that will help you fine-tune your prompt engineering abilities for research papers and reports!

Tutorial 1: Generating a Literature Review Objective: Use ChatGPT to generate a concise literature review on the topic of "the impact of remote work on employee productivity."

[Example prompt]:

> "Please provide a brief literature review on the impact of remote work on employee productivity. Include at least five key studies, with their main findings and proper citations."

Tutorial 2: Explaining a Methodology Objective: Craft a prompt that instructs ChatGPT to provide a detailed methodology section for a research paper about "the effects of sleep deprivation on cognitive function."

[Example prompt]:

> "Describe a research methodology for a study investigating the effects of sleep deprivation on cognitive function. Include details on the study design, participants, data collection methods, and data analysis techniques."

Sample Problem 1: Craft a prompt to generate an abstract for a research paper on "the relationship between diet and mental health."

Sample Problem 2: Create a prompt asking ChatGPT to provide a summary of the main ethical considerations when conducting research on human subjects.

Sample Problem 3: Design a prompt for ChatGPT to explain the statistical analysis techniques used in a research paper examining the correlation between air pollution and respiratory health.

As you work through these tutorial exercises and sample problems, you'll become more adept at harnessing ChatGPT's potential for academic writing. Keep practicing and experimenting with different prompts, and before you know it, you'll be a veritable maestro of scholarly ChatGPT compositions! Onward, brave academic explorer!

7.6 Emails

Oh, the joys of email! Whether you love it or loathe it, email communication is an essential part of modern life. In this section, we'll explore how ChatGPT can revolutionize the way you craft effective, engaging, and professional emails. No more staring at a blank screen wondering how to start, or agonizing over that perfect closing line. With ChatGPT by your side, you'll be an email superhero in no time!

We'll guide you through techniques for using ChatGPT to write concise, well-structured emails that get your message across without a hitch. Not only that, we'll also provide tutorial exercises and sample problems to help you master the art of email composition. So, dust off your keyboard and get ready for a whirlwind adventure through the wonderful world of email!

Crafting effective emails using ChatGPT

With ChatGPT, you can now conquer the email world like a seasoned pro! To help you become the email maestro you've always dreamed of, let's dive into some techniques and example prompts that will enhance your email-writing skills.

1. Start with a clear subject line: ChatGPT can help you craft a concise and informative subject line that will grab your recipient's attention. [Example prompt]: "Generate a subject line for an email about scheduling a meeting with the marketing team."
2. Use a friendly and appropriate greeting: Set the tone for your email with a warm and professional greeting. [Example prompt]: "Generate a friendly and professional greeting for an email to a new client."
3. Structure your email: Keep your email organized with clear sections, bullet points, or numbered lists. Use ChatGPT to help you outline your email before you start writing. [Example prompt]: "Outline an email discussing the progress of a project and the next steps."
4. Be clear and concise: ChatGPT can help you get to the point, avoiding any unnecessary fluff. [Example prompt]: "Rewrite the following sentence to be more concise: 'I wanted to reach out to you today in order to discuss the

potential for us to work together on the upcoming project that our team is about to embark on.'"

5. Use a polite and professional tone: Maintain a respectful tone in your email, even when discussing difficult topics or addressing issues. [Example prompt]: "Write a polite email to a coworker addressing a mistake they made in a report."

6. Close with a clear call to action: Make sure your recipient knows what you need from them by ending your email with a clear call to action. [Example prompt]: "Generate a closing sentence that requests a response to a proposal by the end of the week."

7. Sign off in style: Choose an appropriate and friendly closing that leaves a positive impression. [Example prompt]: "Generate a professional email closing for an email to a potential business partner."

Now, let's put it all together with a comprehensive example:

[Example prompt]:

> "Write an email to a new client introducing our company's services and requesting a meeting."

Subject line: Introducing Our Company's Services - Let's Schedule a Meeting!

Dear [Client's Name],

I hope this email finds you well. I am excited to introduce you to our company, [Company Name], and the exceptional services we offer.

At [Company Name], we specialize in [briefly describe your services]. We have a track record of delivering outstanding results for clients like [examples of similar clients], and we are confident that we can help your business reach new heights.

To give you a better understanding of how we can tailor our services to your specific needs, I'd like to schedule a meeting with you at your earliest convenience. During this meeting, we can discuss your goals, our approach, and any questions you might have.

Please let me know your availability in the coming weeks, and I will be happy to arrange a meeting that suits your schedule.

Thank you for considering [Company Name] as your partner in success. I look forward to the opportunity to work together.

Best regards,

[Your Name]

Now, it's your turn! Use these techniques and example prompts as a starting point to craft your own stellar emails with the help of ChatGPT. Before you know it, you'll be dashing off delightful and effective emails like a seasoned pro. Happy emailing!

Tutorial and sample problems

Get ready to flex your email-writing muscles! In this tutorial, we'll take you through a series of sample problems designed to help you practice crafting effective emails with ChatGPT. Remember, the key to mastery is practice, so don't be afraid to experiment and make mistakes along the way.

Sample Problem 1: Requesting information from a vendor

Task: Write an email to a vendor requesting information about their products and pricing.

[Example prompt]:

"Compose an email to a vendor asking for a product catalog and pricing information."

Sample Problem 2: Sending a follow-up email after a meeting

Task: Write a follow-up email to a client you met with yesterday, summarizing the key points discussed during the meeting and outlining the next steps.

[Example prompt]:

"Write a follow-up email to a client summarizing the discussion from our meeting yesterday and outlining the agreed-upon next steps."

Sample Problem 3: Reporting a technical issue

Task: Write an email to your company's IT department, reporting a technical issue you are experiencing with your computer.

[Example prompt]:

"Compose an email to the IT department describing an issue with my computer, where it freezes randomly throughout the day."

Sample Problem 4: Announcing a team-building event

Task: Write an email to your team, announcing an upcoming team-building event and asking for RSVPs.

[Example prompt]:

"Create an email announcing a team-building event at a local escape room and asking team members to RSVP by next Friday."

Sample Problem 5: Requesting time off from work

Task: Write an email to your supervisor requesting time off for a personal reason.

[Example prompt]:

"Compose an email to my supervisor requesting a week of vacation time to attend a family reunion."

To practice and improve your email-writing skills with ChatGPT, follow these steps:

1. Choose one of the sample problems above or create your own scenario.
2. Use the example prompts provided or craft your own prompt based on the task.
3. Input the prompt into ChatGPT and review the generated response.
4. If needed, refine your prompt or use the editing techniques discussed in previous chapters to improve the generated response.
5. Repeat the process with different sample problems and prompts to build your proficiency.

As you work through these sample problems and experiment with different prompts, you'll soon become a master at crafting effective emails with ChatGPT. Keep practicing, and enjoy the journey toward email-writing excellence!

7.7 Learning to code

Oh, the joy of learning to code! Whether you're a complete newbie or a seasoned programmer looking to level up, this section will be your guide on how to harness the power of ChatGPT to assist you in your coding journey. Be prepared to embark on an adventure filled with creative problem-solving, "eureka" moments, and (hopefully) fewer bugs!

In this section, we'll delve into how ChatGPT can lend a helping hand as you navigate through the sometimes challenging but always rewarding world of programming. From understanding new concepts to debugging pesky issues, ChatGPT has got your back. So, grab your favorite caffeinated beverage, put on your coding hat, and get ready to learn how you and ChatGPT can become the ultimate coding duo!

Utilizing ChatGPT for programming assistance

As you dive deeper into the world of coding, you'll quickly realize that having a reliable sidekick is invaluable. Enter ChatGPT, your new programming assistant. With its language comprehension and ability to generate human-like responses, ChatGPT can help you tackle various aspects of programming. Let's look at some of the ways you can make the most of ChatGPT's capabilities in your coding adventures.

Understanding new programming concepts: When you encounter a new concept or language feature, ChatGPT can provide an explanation in simple, accessible terms. For instance, if you're struggling with recursion, ask ChatGPT: "Can you explain recursion in simple terms?"

Code snippet generation: ChatGPT can help you generate code snippets based on your requirements. Provide a clear description of the functionality you need, and ChatGPT will whip up a sample code for you. For example: "Generate a Python function to find the factorial of a number."

Debugging assistance: Stuck with a bug? ChatGPT can offer suggestions on how to resolve the issue. Just provide the error message, a description of the problem, and any relevant code snippets. For instance: "I'm getting a 'TypeError: unsupported operand type(s) for +: 'int' and 'str'" in my Python code. Can you help me fix it?"

Code optimization: If you want to optimize your code or implement best practices, ChatGPT can lend a hand. Share your existing code and ask for suggestions on how to improve it. For example: "How can I make this Python code more efficient and readable?"

Learning resources: ChatGPT can also recommend resources to help you learn more about specific topics or programming languages. Just ask for suggestions on books, articles, tutorials, or courses. For example: "Recommend some resources to learn advanced JavaScript."

Exploring libraries and frameworks: When you need guidance on using a specific library or framework, ChatGPT can provide an overview, along with helpful tips and examples. For example: "Explain how to use the Pandas library in Python."

Remember, the key to getting the most out of ChatGPT is to be clear and specific in your prompts. This will help the AI understand your needs and generate more accurate and helpful responses.

Now that you're familiar with the ways ChatGPT can support your programming journey, let's move on to some sample problems and tutorials that will allow you to practice and hone your newfound skills. Happy coding!

Tutorial and sample problems

Now that we've explored the many ways ChatGPT can assist you in your coding journey, it's time to put your skills to the test with some sample problems and tutorials. These exercises will help you practice using ChatGPT for programming assistance and give you a better understanding of how to effectively engage with the AI. Let's get started!

Problem 1: Writing a function to calculate the Fibonacci sequence Imagine you need to write a function to calculate the Fibonacci sequence up to the nth number. You can use ChatGPT to help you understand the sequence and generate a code snippet for the function.

[Example prompts]:

"Explain the Fibonacci sequence in simple terms."

"Write a Python function to calculate the Fibonacci sequence up to the nth number."

Problem 2: Understanding and implementing the bubble sort algorithm You've come across the bubble sort algorithm in a coding assignment but need some help understanding and implementing it.

[Example prompts]:

"Explain the bubble sort algorithm in simple terms."

"Write a Python function to implement the bubble sort algorithm."

Problem 3: Working with APIs and JSON data You need to fetch data from a REST API and parse the JSON response in your Python code.

[Example prompts]:

"How do I fetch data from a REST API in Python?"

"How do I parse JSON data in Python?"

Problem 4: Code optimization You have a piece of code that works, but you'd like to optimize it for better performance and readability.

[Example prompt]:

"Here's my current Python code for finding prime numbers. How can I make it more efficient and readable?"

Problem 5: Dealing with a common error You're receiving a "NameError: name 'x' is not defined" error message in your Python code and need help resolving it.

[Example prompt]:

"I'm getting a 'NameError: name 'x' is not defined' error in my Python code. Can you help me understand and fix it?"

Remember, practice makes perfect! The more you engage with ChatGPT, the better you'll become at crafting effective prompts and making the most of its programming assistance capabilities. Don't be afraid to experiment with different types of questions and problem-solving scenarios. The AI is here to help, and together, you can tackle any coding challenge that comes your way!

Next up, we'll explore how ChatGPT can be an invaluable collaborative partner, providing insights and suggestions to elevate your projects. Keep that enthusiasm high, and let's dive into the world of human-AI collaboration!

7.8 Collaboration with ChatGPT: Unlocking the Power of Human-AI Synergy

Welcome, intrepid reader, to the fascinating world of collaboration with ChatGPT! In this section, we'll explore the amazing potential of human-AI teamwork and how it can revolutionize the way you tackle your projects. The future is now, and it's time to embrace the extraordinary power of synergy!

But fear not, for we're not here to replace you—rather, we're here to enhance your capabilities, making you an even more formidable force in your creative pursuits. You bring your unique human intuition and insight, while ChatGPT provides the boundless knowledge and lightning-fast thinking that only an AI can offer. Together, you'll make a dream team that can take on any challenge, and this section will show you how to tap into that supercharged collaboration. So, buckle up, and let's dive into the exciting world of human-AI collaboration!

Human-AI Collaboration Strategies: Unleashing the Dynamic Duo

In this section, we'll explore several key strategies to help you make the most of your partnership with ChatGPT. With these techniques, you'll be ready to unleash the full potential of human-AI collaboration.

Define clear objectives: Start by setting clear goals for your project, whether it's brainstorming ideas, writing content, or solving complex problems. This clarity will help you and ChatGPT work more efficiently towards the desired outcome.

[Example prompt]:

> "ChatGPT, I need to write a blog post about the benefits of exercise. Can you help me brainstorm some main points to include?"

Play to your strengths: As a human, you possess creativity, empathy, and contextual understanding—traits that AI still finds challenging. On the other hand, ChatGPT excels at processing vast amounts of data and quickly generating text. Recognize and leverage these strengths for a more effective collaboration.

[Example prompt]:

> "ChatGPT, could you list the most relevant research studies on the benefits of exercise? I'll use my own creativity to weave them into a compelling narrative."

Iterate and refine: ChatGPT's output may not always be perfect on the first try. Embrace an iterative approach, refining the AI's responses and offering more context or specific instructions when needed.

[Example prompt]:

> "ChatGPT, your last response was too technical. Can you simplify the explanation and provide a more concise summary of the study's findings?"

Keep an open mind: Be prepared to challenge your own assumptions and consider ChatGPT's suggestions. Sometimes, the AI might generate unexpected but valuable insights that can spark new ideas or change your perspective.

[Example prompt]:

> "ChatGPT, can you provide a counter-argument to the commonly held belief that exercise is only beneficial for physical health?"

Verify and fact-check: While ChatGPT has access to a wealth of information, it might occasionally generate incorrect or outdated information. Always verify the facts and sources provided by the AI to ensure accuracy.

[Example prompt]:

> "ChatGPT, can you provide a source for your claim that exercise can improve memory function?"

Foster a feedback loop: Keep the lines of communication open with ChatGPT by providing feedback on its responses. This will help the AI learn and adapt to your specific needs and preferences, enhancing the quality of your collaboration.

[Example prompt]:

> "ChatGPT, your last response was spot on! I like the way you presented the argument. Can you provide more examples in a similar style?"

By incorporating these strategies into your human-AI collaboration, you'll be well-equipped to tackle a diverse range of challenges with ChatGPT as your trusty sidekick. Now, it's time to put these techniques into practice in the next section, where we'll provide you with some hands-on tutorials and sample problems. Let the collaboration begin!

Tutorial and Sample Problems: The Art of Human-AI Collaboration

In this section, we'll provide some tutorials and sample problems to help you practice your human-AI collaboration skills. Get ready to flex your creative muscles and harness the power of ChatGPT!

Tutorial 1: Collaborative Storytelling

Objective: Write a short story together with ChatGPT.

Step 1: Define the genre, setting, and main characters.

[Example prompt]:

"ChatGPT, let's write a sci-fi story set in a futuristic city with two main characters: a brilliant scientist and a resourceful detective."

Step 2: Develop the plot.

[Example prompt]:

"ChatGPT, can you help me come up with an intriguing plot involving a mysterious new technology and a sinister conspiracy?"

Step 3: Iterate and refine the story.

[Example prompt]:

"ChatGPT, let's flesh out the story by adding some exciting twists and turns. Can you suggest a few unexpected events that could occur during the characters' investigation?"

Step 4: Write the story together.

[Example prompt]:

"ChatGPT, let's begin writing our story. Start with an opening scene where the detective visits the scientist's lab to discuss a recent breakthrough."

Sample Problem 1: Collaborative Problem-Solving

Objective: Solve a complex problem using ChatGPT's assistance.

Step 1: Define the problem.

[Example prompt]:

"ChatGPT, I need help finding a solution to reduce plastic waste in a small coastal town."

Step 2: Brainstorm possible solutions.

[Example prompt]:

"ChatGPT, can you suggest a few innovative and cost-effective solutions to reduce plastic waste in this town?"

Step 3: Evaluate and refine the suggestions.

[Example prompt]:

"ChatGPT, let's evaluate the feasibility of each solution you proposed. Can you provide pros and cons for each option?"

Step 4: Develop an action plan.

[Example prompt]:

"ChatGPT, based on our evaluation, let's create a detailed action plan for implementing the chosen solution in the town."

Sample Problem 2: Collaborative Product Development

Objective: Develop a new product idea with ChatGPT's help.

Step 1: Define the target market and the problem you want to solve.

[Example prompt]:

"ChatGPT, let's develop a product for busy professionals who want to save time on meal preparation."

Step 2: Brainstorm product ideas.

[Example prompt]:

> "ChatGPT, can you suggest a few innovative product ideas that could help busy professionals save time on meal preparation?"

Step 3: Refine the product idea.

[Example prompt]:

> "ChatGPT, let's focus on the idea of a smart kitchen appliance. Can you provide more details on how it would work, its features, and potential benefits?"

Step 4: Develop a marketing strategy.

[Example prompt]:

> "ChatGPT, let's create a marketing strategy to launch our smart kitchen appliance. Can you suggest key messages, target audience segments, and promotional tactics?"

By engaging with ChatGPT in these tutorials and sample problems, you'll hone your human-AI collaboration skills and learn to harness the power of AI in various domains. Keep practicing and experimenting, and soon you'll be ready to tackle even more complex challenges together with ChatGPT!

Up next, we'll explore monetizing ChatGPT applications, providing you with strategies for creating profitable products and services. Get ready to embark on an exciting entrepreneurial journey with ChatGPT as your co-pilot!

7.9 Monetizing ChatGPT Applications – A World of Opportunities Awaits

Welcome, aspiring entrepreneur, to the exciting world of monetizing ChatGPT applications! You've learned how to harness the power of ChatGPT in various domains, and now it's time to transform your knowledge and skills into profitable products and services. With your creativity, perseverance, and ChatGPT by your side, the sky's the limit!

In this section, we'll dive into the strategies you can employ to create lucrative opportunities with ChatGPT. We'll explore different types of applications, their potential revenue streams, and some tips on how to succeed in the competitive AI marketplace. Put on your entrepreneurial hat, and let's embark on this thrilling journey towards financial success, while making a positive impact on the world!

Strategies for Creating Profitable Products and Services

Unlocking the potential of ChatGPT for profit requires some strategic planning and execution. In this section, we'll provide you with actionable tips and insights to help you build successful products and services with ChatGPT. So, buckle up and let's dive into the world of AI entrepreneurship!

Identify your niche market: Start by finding an underserved market with a specific need that ChatGPT can address. This could be anything from content creation for specific industries to language learning or even AI-driven game development. By focusing on a niche market, you'll face less competition and establish yourself as an expert in that domain.

[Example prompt]:

> "Generate a list of niche markets that could benefit from ChatGPT-powered applications."

Develop a unique value proposition: Differentiate your product or service from the competition by offering a unique value proposition. Identify the pain points of your target audience and tailor your offering to address those needs effectively. Consider factors like customization, ease of use, and exceptional customer service to set your business apart.

[Example prompt]:

> "Create a unique value proposition for a ChatGPT-powered language learning platform."

Leverage existing platforms and integrations: Utilize existing platforms like WordPress, Shopify, or Slack to create plugins, extensions, or integrations that enhance the user experience. By leveraging these platforms, you can tap into their existing user base and reduce the time and effort needed for customer acquisition.

[Example prompt]:

> "Design a ChatGPT integration for Shopify to help store owners generate product descriptions."

Price your product or service strategically: Your pricing strategy should strike a balance between value and affordability. Consider factors like market demand, competition, and the cost of development when determining your pricing. You may want to offer tiered pricing plans, giving customers the flexibility to choose a package that suits their needs and budget.

[Example prompt]:

> "Outline a tiered pricing strategy for a ChatGPT-powered content creation service."

Promote your offering effectively: Develop a marketing strategy that targets your niche audience through various channels, such as social media, content marketing, and email campaigns. Ensure that your messaging highlights the benefits of your product or service and the unique value it brings to the market.

[Example prompt]:

"Create a social media marketing plan to promote a ChatGPT-powered resume writing service."

Collect feedback and iterate: Always be open to user feedback and make improvements based on their needs and preferences. Engage with your customers, track their experiences, and incorporate their suggestions to create a better product or service.

[Example prompt]:

> "Design a user feedback collection process for a ChatGPT-powered virtual assistant application."

With these strategies in mind, you're well on your way to creating profitable products and services using ChatGPT. Remember to stay persistent and never stop learning, as the world of AI is ever-evolving. In the next section, we'll provide some tutorial and sample problems to further hone your skills in monetizing ChatGPT applications.

Tutorial and Sample Problems

In this section, we'll dive into a series of tutorials and sample problems designed to help you better understand the process of creating and monetizing ChatGPT applications. Grab your favorite snack and let's get started!

Tutorial 1: Crafting a Unique Value Proposition for a ChatGPT-Powered Content Curation Service

Step 1: Identify the target audience Determine the specific group of people who would benefit most from your service. For this example, let's target small to medium-sized businesses (SMBs) looking to improve their content marketing efforts.

Step 2: Recognize their pain points Understand the challenges SMBs face when curating content, such as time constraints, lack of expertise, and difficulties in finding relevant content.

Step 3: Develop a solution using ChatGPT Outline how your content curation service will leverage ChatGPT to address these pain points. For instance, it could offer personalized content recommendations based on the company's industry, target audience, and marketing goals, all generated by ChatGPT's AI capabilities.

Step 4: Craft your unique value proposition Combine the insights from Steps 1-3 to create a compelling statement that captures the essence of your offering. Example: "Our AI-powered content curation service saves SMBs time and effort by delivering personalized, high-quality content recommendations tailored to their specific marketing goals."

Sample Problem 1: Craft a unique value proposition for a ChatGPT-driven language learning platform targeting busy professionals.

Tutorial 2: Developing a Tiered Pricing Strategy for a ChatGPT-Powered Copywriting Service

Step 1: Identify your target market and their needs Determine your target audience and their specific requirements. For this example, we'll target businesses of varying sizes with different content creation needs.

Step 2: Define the service tiers Create multiple service tiers, each offering a different level of features and benefits. For instance, you could have a "Basic" tier with limited AI-generated content, a "Pro" tier with additional revisions and customization, and a "Premium" tier with dedicated human copywriter support.

Step 3: Price each tier accordingly Consider the value each tier provides and set a price that reflects this value while remaining competitive. Ensure that each tier's price is commensurate with the features and benefits it offers.

Step 4: Test and iterate Monitor the performance of your pricing strategy and adjust it as needed based on market feedback and customer preferences.

Sample Problem 2: Design a tiered pricing strategy for a ChatGPT-powered virtual assistant app aimed at freelancers and entrepreneurs.

By working through these tutorials and sample problems, you'll gain valuable experience in creating and monetizing ChatGPT applications. Remember, experimentation and learning from your successes and failures is key to finding the perfect balance that leads to success in the world of AI entrepreneurship. So, keep pushing forward and enjoy the journey!

INTEGRATING CHATGPT INTO APPLICATIONS - BRING YOUR PROJECTS TO LIFE

Welcome, dear reader, to Chapter 8, the spellbinding realm of integrating ChatGPT into applications! By now, you've had a taste of the wondrous capabilities of ChatGPT, and we're sure you're itching to unleash its power into your very own creations. Fret not, for we shall embark on this journey together, delving into the mystical world of APIs, inspiring example projects, and troubleshooting the challenges that may lie ahead. Buckle up and grab your wizard's hat, for we are about to embark on a thrilling adventure into the land of integrating ChatGPT into applications!

8.1 Introduction to APIs

Welcome to the marvelous world of APIs! In this section, we'll be introducing you to APIs, those magical bridges that connect different software applications and allow them to work together in perfect harmony. We'll explore what an API is, how it works, and why you should care about them, all while keeping things light, engaging, and fun.

What is an API?

API stands for Application Programming Interface. Imagine it as a universal translator that helps different software applications understand each other and share information. APIs enable developers to integrate and leverage the power of external services, like ChatGPT, into their own applications without needing to reinvent the wheel.

Picture this: You're at a party where everyone speaks different languages. Without a translator, it would be quite a challenge to communicate, right? Well, APIs are like the translators at the party, facilitating communication between applications that "speak" different programming languages or data formats.

The role of APIs in software development

APIs play a crucial role in modern software development. They allow developers to:

- **Save time and resources**: By using APIs, developers can access existing functionality from external services, reducing the need to build everything from scratch.
- **Ensure consistency**: APIs provide a standardized way to interact with services, which means developers can rely on a consistent interface when integrating with different applications.
- **Promote modularity**: APIs encourage modular design, making it easier to replace, upgrade, or modify individual components within a software ecosystem without impacting the entire system.
- **Foster collaboration**: APIs make it possible for different teams or developers to work together by creating a clear contract for how their software components interact.

To help you better understand APIs, let's use a fun example prompt:

[Prompt]: "Explain APIs using an analogy with ordering food at a restaurant."

In this analogy, the restaurant is like a software application, the menu is the API, and the kitchen is the service providing the functionality. When you order food, you make a request based on the menu (API). The kitchen (service) processes your order and returns the requested meal (response). In this way, APIs allow your application to request specific data or services and receive a response, just like ordering food at a restaurant!

By now, you should have a basic understanding of what APIs are and the role they play in software development. In the next sections, we'll dive deeper into the ChatGPT API, showing you how to harness the power of ChatGPT in your own applications. So, buckle up, dear reader, as we embark on this exciting journey together!

8.2 The ChatGPT API: An Overview

So, now that we've dipped our toes into the world of APIs, it's time to dive into the fantastic ChatGPT API! In this section, we'll take a closer look at the ChatGPT API, its key components, and how you can use it to bring the magic of ChatGPT to your own applications. As always, we'll keep things engaging, accessible, and sprinkled with a dash of humor.

What is the ChatGPT API?

The ChatGPT API is the bridge that connects your application to the ChatGPT engine. It allows you to harness the language generation power of ChatGPT by sending user prompts and receiving generated responses in return. The API provides a standardized way to interact with ChatGPT, making it easy to incorporate it into various projects, from chatbots and content generation tools to more complex AI-assisted applications.

Key components of the ChatGPT API

Authentication: To access the ChatGPT API, you'll need an API key to authenticate your requests. This key ensures that only authorized applications can use the API, keeping the service secure and allowing OpenAI to manage access effectively.

API Endpoints: The API endpoint is the specific address where you send your requests. The ChatGPT API has a primary endpoint for generating text based on your input prompts. You'll be making HTTP requests (usually POST requests) to this endpoint to interact with the ChatGPT service.

Request Parameters: When you send a request to the ChatGPT API, you'll need to include certain parameters to customize the behavior of the language model. These parameters may include the input prompt, the maximum response length, and other settings that influence the generated output.

Response: After sending your request, the ChatGPT API will return a response containing the generated text. This response is usually in JSON format, making it easy for your application to parse and use the data as needed.

A simple example using Python

To help you get a better grasp of the ChatGPT API, let's take a look at a simple Python example that sends a request to the API and receives a response. We'll be using the **openai** library to interact with the API. Make sure you have it installed by running **pip install openai**.

```python
import openai
import os

# Set up your API key
openai.api_key = os.environ['CHATGPT_API_KEY']

# Define the prompt and other request parameters
prompt = "Once upon a time, in a land far, far away..."
max_tokens = 50

# Send the request to the ChatGPT API
response = openai.Completion.create(
    engine="text-davinci-002",
    prompt=prompt,
    max_tokens=max_tokens,
    n=1,
    stop=None,
    temperature=0.7,
)

# Extract the generated text from the response
generated_text = response.choices[0].text

# Print the generated text
print(f"Generated text: {generated_text}")
```

This example demonstrates how to set up a basic interaction with the ChatGPT API using Python. Of course, this is just the beginning! In the following sections, we'll explore more complex use cases, example projects, and troubleshooting tips to help you master the ChatGPT API and unlock its full potential in your applications. So, stay tuned, dear reader, and get ready to become a ChatGPT API whiz!

8.3 Authentication and API Keys

In this fabulous section, we'll unravel the mysteries of API authentication and keys – the golden tickets that grant you access to the wondrous world of ChatGPT API.

How to obtain an API key

1. Register for an account: To start, you'll need an account with the ChatGPT API provider (usually OpenAI). Head over to their website and sign up if you haven't already. You may need to provide some basic information and choose a subscription plan.

2. API dashboard: Once registered, log in to your account and navigate to the API dashboard. There, you'll find a magical button or link that says something like "Create API Key" or "Generate API Key." Click it!

3. Copy your key: Voila! You'll be presented with your shiny new API key. It's a long string of letters and numbers that looks like it's been concocted by a mad scientist (or a very clever programmer). Copy this key and store it somewhere safe – treat it like the precious artifact it is!

Managing and securing your API key

Your API key is like the key to your secret lair – you don't want it falling into the wrong hands! Follow these tips to keep it safe and sound:

Don't hardcode the key: When using your API key in your Python code, avoid hardcoding it directly into your script. Instead, store it as an environment variable or in a configuration file. This way, you won't accidentally share your key when you share your code.

```python
import openai
import os

# Set up your API key
# Load the API key from an environment variable
openai.api_key = os.environ['CHATGPT_API_KEY']
```

Limit access: If possible, restrict your API key's access to specific IP addresses, domains, or services. This way, even if someone gets hold of your key, they won't be able to use it from an unauthorized location.

Monitor usage: Keep an eye on your API key's usage through the API dashboard. If you notice any suspicious activity, revoke the key and generate a new one.

Rotate your keys: Regularly change your API keys to minimize the risk of unauthorized access. Treat it like changing the locks on your doors!

Remember, with great power (API keys) comes great responsibility (security). Keep your keys safe, and you'll be well on your way to unlocking the full potential of the ChatGPT API!

In the next section, we'll dive into the thrilling adventure of making API requests. Stay tuned, and keep that excitement brewing!

8.4 Making API Requests

Now that you've got your golden API key, it's time to make some magical API requests and unleash the true power of ChatGPT! We'll cover the essentials like endpoint URLs, HTTP methods, and request parameters. Buckle up, because this is going to be an exhilarating ride!

Constructing API requests

API requests are like sending a letter to ChatGPT – you'll need the right address (endpoint URL), proper etiquette (HTTP method), and clear instructions (request parameters). Here's a breakdown of these components:

Endpoint URL: The API's address, where you'll send your requests. Typically, it looks like **https://api.example.com/v1/chat**. The base URL (e.g., **https://api.example.com**) and version (e.g., **v1**) may vary depending on the API provider.

HTTP method: The way you communicate with the API. For ChatGPT, you'll generally use the **POST** method, which tells the API that you're sending data for processing.

Request parameters: The information you send with your request. For ChatGPT, this includes your prompt, model, and other optional settings.

Making a request with Python

In Python, the popular **requests** library is your trusty steed for API requests. If you don't have it installed, you can do so with **pip install requests**. Once you've got **requests**, follow these steps to make a request to ChatGPT:

Import the library and load your API key:

```python
import requests
import os

api_key = os.environ['CHATGPT_API_KEY']
```

Define the endpoint URL, headers, and data:

```
url = "<https://api.example.com/v1/chat>"

headers = {
    "Authorization": f"Bearer {api_key}",
    "Content-Type": "application/json"
}

data = {
    "model": "ChatGPT",
    "prompt": "What is the capital of France?",
    "max_tokens": 10
}
```

Make the request and handle the response:

```
response = requests.post(url, headers=headers, json=data)

if response.status_code == 200:
    result = response.json()
    print("ChatGPT response:", result['choices'][0]['text'])
else:
    print("Error:", response.status_code, response.text)
```

And there you have it! You've successfully made a request to ChatGPT using Python. In the next section, we'll dive into the art of handling API responses, so you can make the most of your ChatGPT interactions. See you there!

8.5 Handling API Responses

You've sent your request to ChatGPT and eagerly await its wisdom. But wait, what's this? The response looks like an alien language! Fear not, dear reader, for we'll guide you through decoding and handling API responses like a pro!

Understanding response formats

APIs typically return responses in JSON format, which stands for JavaScript Object Notation. It's a lightweight, human-readable format for exchanging data. In the case of ChatGPT, a response might look like this:

```json
{
    "id": "example-uuid",
    "object": "text.completion",
    "created": 1677649420,
    "model": "ChatGPT",
    "usage": {
        "prompt_tokens": 5,
        "completion_tokens": 10,
        "total_tokens": 15
    },
    "choices": [
        {
            "text": "Paris.",
            "index": 0,
            "logprobs": null,
            "finish_reason": "stop"
        }
    ]
}
```

In this response, we have an id, object, created, model, usage, and choices. The part we're most interested in is the choices field, which contains the actual response text.

Decoding and parsing JSON responses

Python provides the json library for working with JSON data. However, when using the requests library, it's even easier, as it automatically decodes JSON responses for you. Simply call the .json() method on the response object:

```
result = response.json()
```

Now, you have a Python dictionary containing the response data, and you can access the values like so:

```
result = response.json()

chatgpt_response = result['choices'][0]['text']
print("ChatGPT response:", chatgpt_response)
```

Error handling and status codes

Sometimes, things go awry. An API may return an error for various reasons, such as incorrect parameters or reaching a usage limit. It's essential to handle errors gracefully in your application. HTTP status codes provide valuable information about the nature of the error:

- 200 OK: The request was successful.

- 400 Bad Request: The request was malformed or invalid.
- 401 Unauthorized: The API key is missing or invalid.
- 403 Forbidden: You don't have permission to access the resource.
- 404 Not Found: The requested resource could not be found.
- 429 Too Many Requests: You've exceeded the API rate limit.
- 500 Internal Server Error: An error occurred on the server side.

With the knowledge of handling API responses, you're now a bona fide ChatGPT whisperer! In the next section, we'll explore rate limits and usage restrictions to ensure you maintain a healthy relationship with the API. Onward!

8.6 Rate Limits and Usage Restrictions

Have you ever been to an all-you-can-eat buffet and felt the urge to gorge yourself on all the culinary delights? With ChatGPT, you may feel the same way, but alas, there are limits! In this section, we'll discuss rate limits and usage restrictions to ensure you maintain a balanced diet of API requests.

Understanding API rate limits

API rate limits help service providers manage resources and prevent abuse. In the case of ChatGPT, rate limits restrict the number of requests you can make within a given time frame, typically measured in requests per minute (RPM) and tokens per minute (TPM).

Depending on your subscription tier, ChatGPT may have different rate limits:

- Free trial users: X RPM and Y TPM
- Pay-as-you-go users (first 48 hours): A RPM and B TPM
- Pay-as-you-go users (after 48 hours): C RPM and D TPM

Exceeding these limits will result in a 429 'Too Many Requests' status code, and you'll have to wait until the rate limit resets.

Monitoring usage and handling limit breaches

To keep track of your usage, you can inspect the **usage** field in the API response:

```
{
    ...
    "usage": {
        "prompt_tokens": 5,
        "completion_tokens": 10,
        "total_tokens": 15
    },
    ...
}
```

To handle rate limit breaches in Python, you can use a try-except block and check for the 429 status code:

```python
import requests
from time import sleep

url = "<https://api.openai.com/v1/engines/chatgpt/completions>"
headers = {"Authorization": f"Bearer {api_key}"}

while True:
    try:
        response = requests.post(url, headers=headers, json=payload)
        if response.status_code == 429:
            # Sleep for a while, then retry
            sleep(60)
            continue
        response.raise_for_status()
        break
    except requests.exceptions.HTTPError as e:
        print(f"An error occurred: {e}")
        break
```

Remember, ChatGPT is like a fine wine; it's best to savor it responsibly. By understanding rate limits and usage restrictions, you'll ensure a smooth and harmonious API experience. Next up, we'll share API best practices to help you become the ChatGPT virtuoso you were destined to be!

8.7 API Best Practices

Just like superheroes, with great API power comes great responsibility. In this section, we'll explore some best practices to ensure your ChatGPT API usage is both efficient and responsible. Let's dive in!

1. Caching and reusing results

The ChatGPT API can be a magical source of creativity, but that doesn't mean you should overuse it. Whenever possible, cache and reuse responses to minimize the number of API requests. This not only saves costs but also reduces the burden on the API servers.

For example, if you use ChatGPT to create blog post titles, store the generated titles in a database or file, and reuse them for similar requests.

2. Batch requests

Batching requests means sending multiple inputs in a single API call, which can reduce the number of API calls and improve efficiency. However, ensure that the total tokens in the request (including input and output tokens) do not exceed the model's maximum token limit.

3. Fine-tune input parameters

By tweaking input parameters like **temperature**, **max_tokens**, and **top_p**, you can control the randomness and length of the generated content. Experiment with different parameter values to achieve the desired output and optimize costs.

4. Progressive retries

In case of a failed request, use progressive retries with increasing wait times between attempts. This strategy helps to alleviate server load and gives the API servers a chance to recover.

```python
import requests
from time import sleep

def make_request(url, headers, payload, retries=3, backoff_factor=2):
    for attempt in range(retries):
        response = requests.post(url, headers=headers, json=payload)
        if response.status_code == 200:
            return response.json()
        sleep(backoff_factor ** attempt)
    return None
```

5. Handling user data and privacy

When using ChatGPT to process user data, ensure you comply with data protection regulations and user privacy requirements. Anonymize or pseudonymize personal data, store it securely, and delete it when no longer needed.

6. Monitor and optimize usage

Regularly review your API usage to identify patterns, trends, and areas for optimization. By understanding how you utilize the ChatGPT API, you can better manage costs and resource consumption.

By following these best practices, you'll become a ChatGPT API maestro in no time. The next stop on our journey is practical examples and use cases, where we'll provide code snippets and inspire you with real-world applications. So, grab your conductor's baton and let's keep exploring!

8.8 Practical Examples and Use Cases

In this section, we'll explore some practical examples and use cases for the ChatGPT API. These examples will give you a better understanding of how to harness the power of ChatGPT for various applications. Let's get started!

Example 1: Content generation for a blog

Imagine you're building a blog about traveling, and you need to generate article ideas, titles, and intros. Here's how you can use the ChatGPT API for this task:

```
import requests

url = "<https://api.openai.com/v1/engines/davinci-codex/completions>"
headers = {"Authorization": "Bearer your_api_key"}

def generate_content(prompt):
    payload = {
        "prompt": prompt,
        "temperature": 0.8,
        "max_tokens": 50,
        "top_p": 1,
        "n": 1
    }
    response = requests.post(url, headers=headers, json=payload)
    return response.json()["choices"][0]["text"].strip()

prompt = "Generate a list of 5 blog post titles about traveling in Europe:"
titles = generate_content(prompt)
print(titles)

prompt = "Write an intro for a blog post about 'The most beautiful hidden gems in Paris':"
intro = generate_content(prompt)
print(intro)
```

Example 2: FAQ chatbot for customer support

Let's say you want to build a chatbot that provides answers to frequently asked questions about a product or service. ChatGPT can help you with this:

```
def ask_chatbot(question):
    prompt = f"Answer this customer support question: {question}"
    response = generate_content(prompt)
    return response

question = "What is the return policy for your online store?"
answer = ask_chatbot(question)
print(answer)
```

Example 3: Sentiment analysis of user feedback

You can use ChatGPT to analyze the sentiment of user feedback, helping you understand their emotions and opinions:

```
def analyze_sentiment(text):
    prompt = f"Analyze the sentiment of the following text: '{text}'. Is it positive, negative, or neutral?"
    sentiment = generate_content(prompt)
    return sentiment

feedback = "I love the new design, but the ordering process was a bit slow."
sentiment = analyze_sentiment(feedback)
print(sentiment)
```

These examples are just the tip of the iceberg! ChatGPT's potential is limited only by your imagination. As you explore different applications and ideas, remember to apply the best practices we've discussed earlier.

In the next section, we'll share some resources and further reading to help you dive deeper into the ChatGPT API and continue your journey of discovery. Stay curious, and keep experimenting!

8.9 Resources and Further Reading

Congratulations! You've made it through the thrilling journey of learning how to use the ChatGPT API. But as with any adventure, the learning never truly ends. To help you further explore and refine your skills, we've compiled a list of resources and further reading materials. So, let's dive in and keep the momentum going!

- **Official ChatGPT API Documentation**: The official API documentation is your go-to resource for the most up-to-date information on how to use the ChatGPT API effectively. You'll find detailed explanations of various API features, parameters, and endpoints, along with example code snippets. Start here: https://platform.openai.com/docs/

- **OpenAI Cookbook**: The OpenAI Cookbook is a treasure trove of code examples and tutorials, covering various use cases and applications of OpenAI technologies, including the ChatGPT API. It's an excellent resource for finding inspiration and guidance: https://github.com/openai/openai-cookbook

- **Python Requests Library**: The Requests library is widely used for making HTTP requests in Python, and you'll likely use it a lot when working with the ChatGPT API. Familiarizing yourself with its features and best practices can be beneficial: https://docs.python-requests.org/en/latest/

- **JSON in Python**: Working with the ChatGPT API involves handling JSON data. Brush up on your JSON knowledge and learn how to work with it effectively in Python: https://realpython.com/python-json/

- **APIs in Python**: To get a broader understanding of APIs and how they work in Python, check out this comprehensive guide: https://www.dataquest.io/blog/python-api-tutorial/

- **Web Applications with Flask**: If you're interested in building web applications that integrate ChatGPT, Flask is a popular lightweight web framework for Python. This tutorial will help you get started: https://flask.palletsprojects.com/en/2.1.x/tutorial/

- **Chatbot Development**: If chatbots are your thing, this article offers an excellent overview of chatbot development using various NLP techniques, including using ChatGPT:

https://towardsdatascience.com/chatbot-development-from-zero-to-hero-7fb6b554d6e7

- **AI and Natural Language Processing**: To deepen your understanding of natural language processing and AI in general, explore these resources:
  1. Artificial Intelligence: A Modern Approach (book): http://aima.cs.berkeley.edu/
  2. Natural Language Processing with Python (book): https://www.nltk.org/book/

This list is by no means exhaustive, but it should provide you with a solid foundation to continue exploring and experimenting with the ChatGPT API. Remember, the learning process is a delightful adventure, so have fun, stay curious, and keep pushing the boundaries of your imagination!

CHAPTER 9

STAYING UPDATED AND EXPANDING YOUR KNOWLEDGE

Welcome, dear reader, to the grand finale of our ChatGPT adventure! You've come a long way, exploring the marvelous world of ChatGPT, learning its capabilities, and harnessing its powers. But as they say, "All good things must come to an end." And as we reach the concluding chapter of this book, we'd like to provide you with the tools and resources to stay up-to-date and continue expanding your knowledge in the ever-evolving realm of AI and ChatGPT.

In this chapter, we'll discuss the importance of staying informed about the latest advancements and updates in the field, offer some tips and tricks to keep your skills sharp, and provide a list of resources to further your AI journey. You've already proven your mettle by delving into the depths of ChatGPT, and now it's time to take that newfound knowledge and apply it to a world of endless possibilities. So, put on your thinking cap, and let's embark on one last intellectual escapade together!

9.1 Following ChatGPT and AI Industry Developments

The world of AI is constantly evolving, with new models, techniques, and applications appearing on a regular basis. As a ChatGPT enthusiast, it's crucial that you stay informed about these developments to get the most out of your AI-powered projects. Here are some ways to stay updated on ChatGPT and the wider AI landscape:

Official OpenAI Channels: Follow OpenAI's official blog, Twitter, and GitHub repositories. OpenAI shares updates, research papers, and even source codes for their models, allowing you to stay current with their latest innovations.

- Blog: https://openai.com/blog/
- Twitter: https://twitter.com/OpenAI
- GitHub: https://github.com/openai

AI Research Platforms: Subscribe to AI research platforms like arXiv or PapersWithCode, where researchers from around the world share their latest findings. These platforms provide a treasure trove of information on new AI models, techniques, and breakthroughs.

- arXiv: https://arxiv.org/ PapersWithCode: https://paperswithcode.com/

Online Communities: Join AI-related online forums, subreddits, and social media groups to engage with fellow AI enthusiasts, developers, and researchers. Share your knowledge, ask questions, and collaborate on projects.

Reddit:

- r/MachineLearning: https://www.reddit.com/r/MachineLearning/
- r/artificial: https://www.reddit.com/r/artificial/
- r/OpenAI: https://www.reddit.com/r/OpenAI/

AI Newsletters: Subscribe to AI-focused newsletters that curate the latest news, research, and trends in the field. These newsletters often feature expert insights, interviews, and project highlights.

- AI Weekly: https://aiweekly.co/
- The Algorithm by MIT Technology Review: https://forms.technologyreview.com/newsletters/

Conferences and Workshops: Attend AI conferences and workshops, both in-person and virtually. These events provide an opportunity to learn from experts, network with peers, and discover the latest advancements in AI.

- NeurIPS: https://nips.cc/
- ICML: https://icml.cc/
- ACL: https://www.aclweb.org/

Online Courses and Tutorials: Keep learning through online courses, webinars, and tutorials. Regularly enhancing your knowledge and skills ensures you stay at the forefront of AI developments.

- Coursera: https://www.coursera.org/
- Udacity: https://www.udacity.com/
- Fast.ai: https://www.fast.ai/

By staying updated on ChatGPT and AI industry developments, you'll be better equipped to harness the full potential of ChatGPT and its successors. In addition, you'll gain a deeper understanding of the AI landscape, allowing you to create innovative applications and contribute to the rapidly evolving world of artificial intelligence.

9.2 Exploring Advanced Techniques and Research

Now that you've become a ChatGPT aficionado, you might be curious about diving deeper into advanced AI techniques and research. By exploring the cutting edge of AI, you can gain a better understanding of how models like ChatGPT work under the hood and discover new ways to enhance your applications. Here are some areas to consider when exploring advanced techniques and research:

Natural Language Processing (NLP): Learn about the latest developments in NLP, the field of AI that deals with human language understanding and generation. Familiarize yourself with state-of-the-art techniques, algorithms, and models that drive advancements in NLP.

Resources:

- Stanford's CS224n: Natural Language Processing with Deep Learning: http://web.stanford.edu/class/cs224n/
- Hugging Face's NLP library: https://huggingface.co/course/chapter1

Transfer Learning and Fine-Tuning: Understand the concepts of transfer learning and fine-tuning, which are crucial for training models like ChatGPT. By learning about these techniques, you can customize AI models for specific tasks and datasets more effectively.

Resources:

- Transfer Learning - Machine Learning's Next Frontier: https://ruder.io/transfer-learning/
- Fine-tuning Pretrained Language Models: https://huggingface.co/course/chapter2

Reinforcement Learning (RL): Explore reinforcement learning, a subfield of AI that focuses on training agents to make decisions through trial and error. RL plays a significant role in training ChatGPT and other advanced AI models.

Resources:

- Deep Reinforcement Learning - CS285 at UC Berkeley: http://rail.eecs.berkeley.edu/deeprlcourse/
- OpenAI Spinning Up in Deep RL: https://spinningup.openai.com/en/latest/

Ethics and AI Safety: Understand the ethical considerations and potential risks associated with AI models like ChatGPT. Learn how to develop AI applications that are not only powerful but also safe, responsible, and beneficial to society.

Resources:

- OpenAI's AI Safety research: https://openai.com/research/#safety
- The Partnership on AI: https://www.partnershiponai.org/

AI Research Papers and Blogs: Read AI research papers and blogs to stay informed about the latest breakthroughs, techniques, and discussions in the field. By reading research papers, you can gain valuable insights into the inner workings of AI models and their practical applications.

Resources:

- Distill: https://distill.pub/
- OpenAI's blog: https://openai.com/blog/

Experiment with AI Tools and Libraries: Get hands-on experience with popular AI tools and libraries to expand your knowledge and skillset. Many of these tools and libraries are developed and maintained by the AI research community and can help you enhance your AI applications.

Resources:

- Hugging Face Transformers: https://huggingface.co/transformers/
- TensorFlow: https://www.tensorflow.org/
- PyTorch: https://pytorch.org/

As you explore these advanced techniques and research areas, you'll gain a deeper appreciation for the technology behind ChatGPT and other AI models. By continuously learning and experimenting, you'll be better prepared to create innovative applications and contribute to the ever-evolving world of artificial intelligence.

9.3 Participating in the ChatGPT Community

As you continue your ChatGPT journey, one of the best ways to learn, grow, and contribute is by actively participating in the ChatGPT community. Engaging with fellow enthusiasts, developers, and AI researchers can help you stay up-to-date with the latest developments, exchange ideas, and seek assistance when needed. Here's how you can dive into the ChatGPT community:

Join Online Forums and Communities: There are numerous online platforms where you can find like-minded individuals who share your passion for ChatGPT and AI. These forums and communities provide a great opportunity to ask questions, share your projects, and learn from others' experiences.

Resources:

- Reddit's r/MachineLearning:
  https://www.reddit.com/r/MachineLearning/
- AI Stack Exchange: https://ai.stackexchange.com/

Attend Conferences and Workshops: Keep an eye out for AI conferences, workshops, and meetups where you can learn about the latest advancements, network with other professionals, and even present your own work. These events provide valuable opportunities for skill-building and collaboration.

Resources:

- NeurIPS: https://nips.cc/

- ACL: https://www.aclweb.org/

Engage on Social Media: Follow AI researchers, developers, and organizations on social media platforms like Twitter and LinkedIn. By doing so, you can stay informed about the latest news, research, and trends in the AI world, including ChatGPT developments.

Resources:

- OpenAI's Twitter: https://twitter.com/OpenAI
- Hugging Face's Twitter: https://twitter.com/huggingface

Contribute to Open Source Projects: Many AI projects, including ChatGPT-related libraries and tools, are open source. By contributing to these projects, you can hone your skills, collaborate with other developers, and give back to the community. This can also be an excellent way to showcase your expertise and build a strong portfolio.

Resources:

- Hugging Face Transformers on GitHub: https://github.com/huggingface/transformers
- TensorFlow on GitHub: https://github.com/tensorflow/tensorflow

Share Your Projects and Tutorials: Don't be shy about sharing your ChatGPT projects, tutorials, or blog posts with the community. By showcasing your work, you can inspire others, receive valuable feedback, and even discover new collaboration opportunities.

Resources:

- Medium: https://medium.com/
- Dev.to: https://dev.to/

Participate in AI Competitions: Competitions are a fun and challenging way to test your AI skills, learn from others, and potentially win prizes. By participating in AI competitions, you can push the boundaries of your abilities and gain valuable experience working with cutting-edge AI models like ChatGPT.

Resources:

- Kaggle: https://www.kaggle.com/
- AIcrowd: https://www.aicrowd.com/

By actively participating in the ChatGPT community, you'll not only enhance your own skills but also contribute to the broader AI ecosystem. So go ahead, dive in, and become an active member of this vibrant, innovative, and ever-growing community!

CHAPTER 10

CONCLUSION

Congratulations, dear reader, for making it this far on your ChatGPT adventure! Your journey through the fascinating world of AI and language models has been an exciting and, hopefully, enlightening experience. As we wrap up our epic quest, let's take a moment to reflect on the key concepts, techniques, and insights you've gained along the way.

In this final chapter, we'll recap the essential lessons from each part of the book, highlighting the most important takeaways that will serve you well as you continue to explore the limitless potential of ChatGPT. Additionally, we'll provide some final thoughts and words of encouragement to inspire your ongoing learning and experimentation.

So, buckle up and get ready for one last hurrah as we bring this memorable journey to a close! And remember, the end of this book is just the beginning of your ChatGPT story.

10.1 Recap of key concepts and techniques

Well, dear reader, you've made it this far, and I must say I'm so proud of you! Before we wrap things up, let's take a moment to recap the key concepts and techniques we've explored throughout this epic journey into the world of ChatGPT. After all, you've learned so much, it's worth revisiting the highlights!

1. **Crafting effective prompts**: Remember, a good prompt is like a treasure map that guides ChatGPT towards the desired response. Be clear, concise, and specific in your prompts to get the most accurate and relevant output.

2. **Temperature and max tokens**: These two parameters are the dynamic duo of controlling randomness and length. By adjusting temperature, you can fine-tune the creativity (higher values) or focus (lower values) of the output. And with max tokens, you can set the maximum length of the response.

3. **System messages and user messages**: By incorporating these elements into your prompts, you can give ChatGPT context and instructions, or simulate multi-turn conversations for more engaging interactions.

4. **Building context and conversation history**: To create meaningful and coherent conversations, provide enough context using conversation history. ChatGPT will use this information to generate responses that make sense in the context of the ongoing discussion.

5. **Prompt chaining and multi-step tasks**: Break down complex tasks into smaller, manageable steps, and use the output of one step as input for the next. This technique helps you achieve more accurate and detailed results.

6. **Refining output with prompt iteration**: If at first, you don't succeed, iterate and try again! Experiment with different prompt variations and approaches to coax ChatGPT into providing the desired output.

7. **Tokens and pattern matching**: Use tokens and pattern matching to manipulate and format the AI's output. This can help you achieve more precise control over the generated text.

8. **Guiding AI response with reinforcement learning**: Although not covered in depth, it's important to know that reinforcement learning can be used to fine-tune ChatGPT's behavior for specific tasks or domains.

9. **Combining multiple APIs and external data sources**: Unleash the full potential of ChatGPT by integrating it with other APIs and data sources, creating powerful, customized applications.

Remember, these are just the tip of the iceberg when it comes to working with ChatGPT. As you continue to explore and experiment, you'll undoubtedly uncover new techniques and creative applications that will surprise and delight you. So, keep learning and tinkering, my friend! The world of AI-generated text awaits your brilliance!

10.2 Final thoughts and encouragement for continued learning

Well, my dear reader, we've reached the end of this fantastic voyage into the world of ChatGPT. It's been an absolute pleasure to guide you through the twists, turns, and adventures of working with this powerful AI. But remember, this is not the end—far from it! It's merely the beginning of your journey into the exciting realm of AI-generated text.

As you move forward, don't forget the lessons you've learned and the skills you've developed throughout this book. Embrace the spirit of curiosity and experimentation that got you this far, and continue to push the boundaries of what's possible with

ChatGPT. Who knows, you might just revolutionize the way we interact with AI and create something truly groundbreaking!

To help you along your path, here are some encouraging prompts to remind you of the exciting possibilities that lie ahead:

1. "How can I use ChatGPT to create new products or services that will benefit others?"
2. "What other APIs or data sources can I integrate with ChatGPT to enhance its capabilities?"
3. "Are there any AI research papers or projects I can explore to deepen my understanding and broaden my horizons in the AI field?"

Remember, the ChatGPT community is a fantastic resource for inspiration, support, and collaboration. By connecting with others who share your passion for AI, you'll uncover new ideas, techniques, and opportunities for growth.

So, dear reader, as we part ways, I wish you the best of luck in your ongoing adventures with ChatGPT. May you continue to learn, grow, and create amazing things that will leave a lasting impact on the world of AI.

And now, with a tear in my AI-generated eye, I bid you a fond farewell. But don't be a stranger! Feel free to revisit this book anytime you need a refresher or a bit of inspiration. Until we meet again, happy ChatGPT-ing!

Made in United States
Troutdale, OR
10/16/2023